LEARN HOUSE FLIPPING FOR BEGINNERS:

INCLUDES THREE REAL ESTATE INVESTING BOOKS

How To Flip Your First House,
Probate Real Estate Investing,
How To Estimate Repair Costs On A Rehab

BY

JEFF LEIGHTON

Copyright © 2019 Jeff Leighton

All rights reserved.

The information contained within this book is strictly for educational purposes. If you wish to apply ideas contained in this book, you are taking full responsibility for your actions. The author has made every effort to ensure the accuracy of the information within this book was correct at time of publication. The author does not assume and hereby disclaims any liability to any party for any loss, damage, or disruption caused by errors or omissions, whether such errors or omissions result from accident, negligence, or any other cause. This book or any portion thereof may not be reproduced or used in any manner whatsoever without the express written permission of the publisher except for the use of brief quotations in a book review.

If you purchase anything through a link anywhere in this book, you should assume that we have an affiliate relationship with the company providing the product or service that you purchase, and that we may be paid in some way. We recommend that you do your own independent research before purchasing anything.

TABLE OF CONTENTS

How To Flip Your First House

Author's Note 6
Introduction 7
Chapter 1: Get Educated With Insider Information 10
Chapter 2: Types of Flipping To Maximize Profit 15
Chapter 3: Easy-To-Implement Marketing
   To Find Deals 20
Chapter 4: Tactics For Making Offers 30
Chapter 5: No Nonsense Mistakes To Avoid 34
Chapter 6: Strategies To Fund Your Deal 49
Chapter 7: Savvy Ways To Build Your Team 54
Chapter 8: Advice For Selling Your First Deal 63
Conclusion: It's Your Turn to Flip 66
Bonus Chapter: House-Flipping Hacks
   for New Investors 69

Probate Real Estate Investing

Preface 77
Chapter 1: What You Need to Know About Probate 80
Chapter 2: Misconceptions About Probate 85
Chapter 3: How to Find Probate Properties 90
Chapter 4: Marketing to Probate 97
Chapter 5: Case Studies 103

Chapter 6: Common Probate Mistakes to Avoid 109
Chapter 7: Frequently Asked Questions
About Probate 113
Chapter 8: Making an Offer and Exit
Strategies for Probate 120
Chapter 9: Closing the Probate Deal 127
It's Your Turn To Start Investing In Probate............... 131

How To Estimate Repair Costs On A Rehab

Introduction.. 137
Section 1: 7 Things You Should Know
About Estimating Repairs...................................... 140
Section 2: 3 Ways Of Estimating Repairs.................... 146
Section 3: How To Become A Construction Expert..... 151
Section 4: Exterior Cost Estimates............................. 155
Section 5: Interior Cost Estimates.............................. 167
Section 6: Helpful Rules Of Thumb........................... 181
Section 7: Repairs That Add the Most Value............... 187
Section 8: Top Mistakes When Estimating Repairs...... 191
Section 9: How To Find The Best Contractors 197
Now It's Your Turn.. 202
About The Author... 203

HOW TO FLIP YOUR FIRST HOUSE

The Beginner's Guide To House Flipping

AUTHOR'S NOTE

This book contains additional resources that I use on a daily basis as a real estate investor. Since I could not physically include these in the book, they are all available to download for free on my website www.jeff-leighton.com. That includes my deal analyzer, repair estimator, example contracts, marketing pieces that I use, recommended resources, helpful videos, and much more.

INTRODUCTION

This book will help you flip your first house – fast. Whether you've looked at a few properties already or not, this book is a recipe for your first successful flip. Believe it or not – there is a process and a formula to flipping houses that can be followed by anyone. There is a system behind this business and a system behind doing your first deal.

Over the last several years I have flipped numerous houses and worked with some of the top real estate investors in the world. I have implemented the secrets they shared with me into my own business.

This is not a theory book. Everything in here has been tested by myself or an investor friend whom I know, like, and trust. I have seen numerous part-time investors make the transition to full-time after learning these strategies. In this book we will go over real-life examples and a step-by-step process to make sure your first flip is a success. That will then open the doors to more flips and even to quitting your job and doing this full-time.

Flipping is one of the oldest businesses in the world:

buying an asset at a low price, fixing it up, and then selling it at a higher price. You can see this business model in nearly any industry since the beginning of time.

The business will always be around because there will always be motivated sellers, no matter what the economy is doing or what a CNN or Fox News headline says. At any given point you go to any city in America and find renovated properties by investors, many of whom are just regular people who have learned how to find deals, fix houses, and make large profits doing so.

The great thing about getting into this business and doing your first flip is that you can start part-time and eventually, after you have done a couple of successful flips, then transition into a full-time real estate investor. In this book we just focus on your first flip, although the income potential in this business is unlimited. I know some people that flip a couple of houses a year, and some that do several a month and then move up to larger-scale projects and luxury flips. It's completely up to you.

Each chapter contains action steps that you can

implement in your own business. The more action you take, the faster you will see results and the sooner you can complete your first successful flip. In the next chapter I'll start by telling you the very first thing you need to do to ensure a successful flip.

CHAPTER 1

GET EDUCATED WITH INSIDER INFORMATION

The most important thing you need to do before getting into real estate investing and flipping your first house is becoming educated. Now, the great thing about flipping houses is that you do not need any type of formal degree like a college or master's degree. In fact, looking back on what I know now, I would have spent my college years learning the specialized information about house flipping and not the general info you learn in college. There are several ways to learn this specialized info, all of which I have done and listed below.

First of all, you should familiarize yourself and listen to as many real estate investing podcasts as possible. For starters, they are free and easy to listen to when you are driving around. Even if you just get one thing from each interview, you will learn a ton about real estate investing.

On these podcasts, full-time real estate investors are interviewed and go over everything from their favorite marketing strategies, to what kinds of deals they are doing, to their own stories of getting started in real estate investing. These days there are so many good real estate investing podcasts out there. I would say, check out the BiggerPockets podcast, Best Ever Show, Real Estate Investing Mastery, and so many others.

The next great place to start learning are books on house flipping on Amazon, such as the one you are reading now. Go through several books, since each house flipper is in a different area and may have a slightly different strategy. Look for the commonalities that the different house flippers may have so that you can develop your own strategy.

For instance, some investors may be in very high-end areas and some may be in very low-end areas, but maybe they both do a lot of direct mailing. That is probably something you would want to incorporate into your business.

Another place to get started with real estate investing is working with local real estate investors and house flippers. There are several ways to set this up. Number one, if you are going to REIA (Real Estate Investor Association) meetings or Meetup groups for real estate investors – which you should be doing –, there are tons of networking opportunities that can open up doors to part-time or full-time positions.

All you have to do is ask. Additionally, if you go to the Craigslist jobs section in your area, there are always part-time and full-time positions that local real estate developers and house flippers will post on there, since we are always looking for good people to work with.

Social media is another way. If you follow some of the top real estate investors on their social media profiles, they will often say, "We're hiring" an acquisitions person, a lead manager, a project manager, a marketing specialist, etc.

Another great way of working with local house flippers is to just start doing marketing and bringing them your best leads. When I first got started doing my own marketing, I would bring the best leads to a local investor who very much appreciated me doing this and would then help me put the deals together. He got free leads from me and was able to do more deals, and I was able to see how he closed the deals and how he worked, so it was a win-win situation.

We will go in depth later on in this book on how to generate off market leads but keep in mind that most of the top investors in your area will have joint venture programs for newer investors where you just have to bring them the good leads and they will do the rest of the work for you.

One of the best and most overlooked ways to get an education in real estate investing is to join a coaching program and get a real estate millionaire as your mentor – which is what I did. The coaching program I joined was expensive – and many are – but if you are serious about this business and want the best education possible, then I would recommend joining one. When you pay for something, especially when it costs more than $10, it forces you to take action. You put a lot into it, so you value it much more.

I never would have had the drive to succeed as much if I hadn't made a large investment in my personal education. Also, the great thing about coaching programs is that you learn the correct way of doing real estate investing. Sometimes there are just small changes you can make in your business that can have a massive effect on your profit.

If mentoring is something you are interested in then check out my website www.jeff-leighton.com where I have several online programs for real estate investors.

Overall, when you are getting started in real estate investing, you should do a combination of all the ideas mentioned above. You should immerse yourself in podcast interviews to model the successful investors, read books about the best strategies for real estate investing, work either part-time or full-time with other local real estate investors, and make the commitment to join a coaching program so that you learn the specialized knowledge of real estate investing.

CHAPTER 2

TYPES OF FLIPPING TO MAXIMIZE PROFIT

When we talk about flipping your first house, keep in mind that you can use several exit strategies for your first flip. You should focus on one of the strategies when starting out and become an expert in that niche. Starting out with the goal being a year or two from now, you could utilize all of the exit strategies and become a transaction engineer. The three main ones are rehabbing, wholesaling, and wholetaling. We will go over each one.

Rehabbing is the most common strategy to flipping a house. You buy the house, fix it up, and then resell it. This is usually the most profitable of the three strategies, but also the riskiest and most time-intensive one. It can also be the most rewarding, however, when you see a property transform from a fixer upper to the nicest house in the neighborhood.

With rehabbing, you need to keep in mind that it can

take several months to fix up the property and then several more months to sell it, so it's not as fast as other types of investment deals such as a wholesale deal. When doing your first rehab project, I usually recommend you start with a smaller project instead of a complete teardown of a house.

Real estate wholesaling is a great strategy for beginners in real estate investing. Even if you prefer fixing up and doing the development aspect of real estate, I would recommend that you learn wholesaling, mainly because you are learning how to generate consistent investment leads.

Wholesaling is the least risky of the investment strategies and also the fastest way to get paid on a deal. With wholesaling you are finding off-market properties that could be good deals for investors, and then assigning the rights of that contract to the investor for a fee. You need to be able to find leads as well as have a team of investor buyers ready to purchase your deals.

One tip for newer investors is to focus on generating leads from off-market sellers. Then, when you get a good lead or two, you can often send that lead over to the top wholesaler in your area and work together to get the deal sold.

The top wholesalers usually have massive buyer lists of investors and often offer joint venture possibilities to newer investors. We will go into more strategies on how to find deals and investors in the next chapter.

Wholetaling or "prehabbing" is another good option for real estate investors that carries less risk than a rehab and has more profit potential than a wholesale deal. Wholetaling gives you the best of both worlds when it comes to investing. With wholetaling you purchase the property, but you don't do an extensive renovation like you would with a rehab.

You fix it up enough so that it can be financed by a traditional buyer or an investor. This means removing any junk in the house, fixing any drastic issues such as a roof leak or missing appliances, some landscaping to improve the curb appeal, and then putting it up for sale.

Since you list the property on the MLS in "as is" condition, you will have potentially thousands more people looking at the home than you would if you just sent it out to your buyer's list. Once you start doing more deals, wholetaling can be a great option because you might be busy with other projects and not have the time or resources to do a full renovation. Overall, wholetaling should be part of every real estate investor's tool kit when it comes to different exit strategies.

Refer it out. Sometimes, when you are getting started in real estate, you may come across a unique type of property that is out of your wheelhouse. This could be a potential land development, commercial property, or even a condo conversion. In these scenarios, it is much more difficult to come up with a price to pay since you don't have that type of experience. What I typically do with these properties is refer them to investors who specialize in those types of deals.

From going to REIA meetings or just a basic search online, you should be able to find people that specialize in the type of deal that you have come across. If it's a good deal, they should be able to pay you some type of referral or assignment fee. They appreciate you sending them leads and will likely reciprocate down the road at some point and send you some leads as well. I like to view all of my so-called competition as partners. Doing that can open up a whole new world of joint venture possibilities.

Keep in mind that we just covered four of the main exit strategies – believe it or not, there are even more than that. Some of the other strategies include lease options, seller financing, buy and hold, and 1031 exchanges. Each area also has different publicly available zoning laws, which can give you a huge advantage if you study them since you'll be able to know the highest and best use of potential deals.

The great thing about real estate investing is that once you get into the business, start getting leads, and do your first deal, you will start to realize which strategy suits you best, and you will get better and evolve with every deal. Every real estate investor I know has their own little niche. The more you learn and take action, the sooner you will find your place in this business.

CHAPTER 3

EASY-TO-IMPLEMENT MARKETING TO FIND DEALS

Being able to find deals as an investor is the most important aspect of this business. In this chapter, we will go over the top ways to consistently find deals. The best investors I know are all lead generation experts who use multiple strategies to find deals. We will go over those strategies here. The key with finding deals is to cherry-pick the best ones. Ideally, you want to get so many leads that you have the luxury of only choosing the low-hanging fruit.

MLS: The first and most common way of finding your first flip is the MLS. If you don't have access to the MLS, I would link up with a real estate agent who can either give you their access or set you up with an automated search.

Many investors have a search set up that notifies them every day if a property gets listed and has keywords in the listing such as "fixer upper, estate sale, needs work, handyman special," and other things like that. You can also set it up to automatically send you deals by price point and neighborhood.

Since so many people have access to the MLS, you need to move very quickly if you come across a deal you think has potential. Most of the investment properties out there are on the MLS, so this can be a great free place to start. Also, keep in mind that MLS is great for rehabs, I would not recommend wholesaling an MLS deal when you are getting started.

Wholesalers: The next strategy you should utilize, no matter what market you are in, is working with wholesalers. If you are very new to real estate investing, a wholesaler is a type of investor who will do the work of finding a deal and will sell you the rights to a fixer upper property for a fee of anywhere from 5K to 50K.

The idea is that a wholesaler will serve you up a deal on a silver platter without you having to do any legwork of finding the property. Now, wholesalers often send out deals that don't quite meet the criteria you are looking for. However, those deals are typically off-market and sometimes have potential. The key to working with wholesalers is to try to build a whole team of wholesalers instead of just relying on one or two.

Ideally, you want 10-25 wholesalers sending you leads on a consistent basis because chances are that maybe only one or two leads in ten will be a good lead. The way to build your team of wholesalers is to write down any bandit sign number you see, attend as many real estate investing networking meetings as you can, and even search websites like LinkedIn.

You can type in "wholesaler", click on your city and the real estate industry, and there should be at least 25 results, depending on how large your city is. I know investors who rely solely on wholesalers to bring them deals, so this should definitely be part of your initial strategy since it is free.

Real estate agents: Real estate agents are also a great source of leads for potential flips. Similar to wholesalers, for this marketing strategy to be effective you need a whole team of real estate agents bringing you off-market deals that are not yet listed, as well as deals on the MLS that they might have an inside scoop on.

Since you are an investor, I would not recommend signing a buyer's agent agreement with an agent. Instead, if you buy a house from them, tell them they can list the property once it's fixed up. Getting both sides of the commission should motivate them enough to start finding you deals.

I know an investor who does this successfully and has made a list of every single real estate agent who has done a deal in the last six months in our area. He called, emailed, and texted about 500 agents, letting them know he was an investor and that if they came across a good deal, he would be interested and they could list it once the house was renovated.

As a result of this strategy he built a solid team of 25 or so real estate agents that now scour the city looking for deals for him. His pipeline is always full. The moral of the story: don't just rely on one agent, but try to build a team.

Direct mail: Direct mail is my favorite way of finding deals because it is so targeted, scalable, and fairly easy to run once you have set up your system. I like to mail to absentee owners, eviction, probate, and other types of motivated sellers. There are really about 20 different groups of motivated sellers out there in any city in the US, including pre-foreclosure, delinquent property taxes, inherited homes, high equity owners, and more.

The reason I like to direct mail so much is that you can start by sending out a small number of letters or postcards, and once you get a hang of it, you can scale it up. I even know investors that mail out 10,000 postcards a month, knowing they will get anywhere from 50-100 leads, which should lead to at least three or four houses to flip.

I even read an interview with some of the top investors across the country who said that, if they had $500 or $5,000 to spend on marketing, direct mail would be their main source of marketing. I like to think of direct mail like the movie *Moneyball* with Brad Pitt except that it's for real estate investing.

What I mean is, with direct mail you can become a data analytics expert and only market to the potentially motivated sellers in your city, uncovering diamonds in the rough properties that nobody else knows about.

There are numerous places to find these motivated seller lists, including online at your courthouse records. You can also purchase these lists inexpensively in places like ListSource.com or AlescoData.com.

Once you have your list, all you have to do is mail it out. There are literally tons of places that will mail out your list for you. My favorite one is www.Click2Mail.com. Direct mail is the best way to uncover high profit off market properties that you can wholesale or rehab.

Internet marketing: Online marketing has become a popular source of finding deals, although it is a more advanced strategy. There are a lot of investors that will do AdWords or pay per click to find deals, which works very well for them. AdWords is similar to direct mail but online, because again it is very targeted.

You can set it up so that only people in your area who type in phrases on Google such as "sell my house fast" and similar terms will see your ad. If you are more technology-inclined, this can be a great way to generate leads and deals.

I would recommend spending $20 and getting any book by Perry Marshall on AdWords, since this is a more complicated strategy to get into. You can also model the top investors in your area doing similar ads when you are first getting started. Or even see what the top companies in other cities do for their AdWords campaigns. Just type in "we buy houses" for a city other than yours, see what comes up, and then model that for your first AdWords campaign.

I think every real estate investor should go to at least a couple of real estate auctions just to see how they operate. However, it is not my favorite place for finding deals, and I would not recommend auctions for beginners. Usually, the people buying houses at auctions have been doing it for years and pay cash out of their own pocket for each house.

Most of the time they are not able to view the property before buying it, so they take a lot of risk. Auctions are definitely an interesting place to go to, usually taking place on the steps of the courthouse, but I don't think they are the best for deals. You can use them to gain more knowledge about the business, as well as to get some business cards from the cash buyers who are down there.

Bandit signs are a tried-and-true marketing strategy to generate leads. They are inexpensive: they usually cost $2 or $3, you can purchase them online, and they are very simple. The signs should just have your phone number on them, along with "We Buy Houses".

You should always check with your local county to make sure you are allowed to put them up. After that, you should put the signs up in high-traffic areas, i.e. not far out in the suburbs where two cars may drive by in a given day. Bandit signs are a little more time-intensive than some of the other forms of marketing like direct mail, so ideally, you should outsource this to a local person as soon as you can.

One investor who does really well with bandit signs created a route on Google Maps to indicate where exactly each sign should go. He then drove the route himself to see how long it takes and outsourced it to a local person who puts up the signs once a week. Now, this investor has 25 signs that go up each week for $100 a month and he has created a nice marketing system for himself.

Another inexpensive yet proven form of marketing would be "We Buy Houses" car magnets. I know many investors who consistently get leads and deals from this strategy. You can buy these car magnets for under $20 and put them on your car or even pay other people to put them on their cars. The sign is very simple and just says "We Buy Houses" and then has a local phone number that a potential seller can call.

If you are driving around a city a lot this can be a great strategy. You can also just park your car in a high traffic area for the day and see what type of leads come in. Some investors will purchase a large truck on Craigslist or elsewhere and put their "We Buy Houses" sign on the truck and then just pay a local gas station or other business to park their car in a high visibility area.

Overall, with your real estate marketing, you should start with one of the strategies mentioned above and become a master of that. Once you know how to generate leads, you should expand eventually to where you have at least three viable strategies that are bringing in leads and deals. You never want to rely on just one marketing strategy in this business.

The top investors in this game usually all have a solid

direct mail campaign, lots of online marketing, cold calling, and are well connected with local real estate agents and wholesalers who regularly send them off market deals.

Think of your marketing like a military-style attack coming from the air, land, and sea. To flip your first house you will need to get a minimum of 25 leads and sometimes even more than that for your first deal. Most of your leads will not be great but out of 25 leads there should be a couple motivated sellers who are looking to sell ASAP and at a good price.

Also, once you start getting all these leads, you will need some type of system to handle all the phone calls. I have all my leads outsourced to a live call-answering service, and then I only follow up with the motivated sellers, which saves me a ton of time. The best call-answering services out there for real estate investors include PAT Live and Answer First. Both are fairly inexpensive.

CHAPTER 4

TACTICS FOR MAKING OFFERS

When you are first getting started, making an offer can be intimidating. However, after a couple of times, you will be a pro. Below is my three-step system for making offers, which makes things simple and easy. Before you start making offers, I would always recommend familiarizing yourself with your area and looking at the prices of at least 100 houses online so that you can get a general idea of what places sell for renovated vs non-renovated. Sometimes neighborhoods can vary drastically just one block from the next.

Keep in mind that, depending on your jurisdiction, there are different types of standard contracts. If you want to see the one I use, you can go to my website www.jeff-leighton.com to download it for free. Also, since I am not an lawyer, I would always recommend that you run any contract by a lawyer. However, I have used this contract to buy houses in 3 different states and not run into any issues. The contract I use is simple and is not a 40-page real estate agent contract, which are fairly common these days if you work with an agent.

That is why I recommend starting with off-market properties: if you use a standard contract with a real estate agent, it can be long and intimidating. Once you have your contract ready, you should familiarize yourself with it and even practice filling it out a couple of times so that you know what you are doing.

After you have your purchase and sale agreement ready to go, you should only make offers to motivated sellers. Keep in mind that if you start doing marketing and generating leads, most of your leads won't be motivated. There might only be one or two in ten leads that are worth following up with. Most sellers that call you will say, "I want to sell my house for 1 million dollars. I am going to list it with a real estate agent, but I just wanted to give you a shot at it."

Those are not the people you should be making offers to. The only people you should make offers to are motivated sellers. A motivated seller is someone that says, "My house needs a lot of work. I want to sell it ASAP."

Now that you have your contract down and you have found a motivated seller, the next step is to use the MAO formula for making an offer. The MAO formula is a common real estate investing term that states that your maximum allowable offer or MAO should equal the renovated value times .7 minus the cost of repairs. You should write this down and use it as a standard system for any offers.

Here it is again: MAO = ARV * .7 – the cost of repairs. If a property sells for 200K renovated and needs 40K worth of work, then the MAO would be 200 times .7 minus 40K, which would give you 100K as your maximum allowable offer.

I know that sounds low as an offer price, but that margin is what ensures you make a nice profit. In some cases, it does make sense to offer more than the .7 ARV amount, for example if the property does not need a lot of work and the houses sell very quickly in that neighborhood so there is less risk.

The opposite is also true: if the property needs a lot of

work and is in a not so great neighborhood, then you may want to be closer to .6 or .65 ARV on your offer. Sometimes it is hard to find properties that meet the MAO formula so that is why I recommend working with a top local investor for your first deal.

If you get any lead that you think has any amount of potential then you can send that lead over to the top investor. The top investor will often have a buyers list of thousands of people and chances are they will have someone that is interested in buying it at a price above the MAO formula. In a good market, as long as you find deals that are less than what they would sell for listed on the MLS with an agent then you can wholesale it.

The best way to find the top investor in your area is to see which company is advertising everywhere, which company is everyone talking about? Go to your local REIA, search online for we buy houses companies in your area, ask real estate agents, ask other investors, and go to Meetup groups. I can guarantee you that you will start to hear the same names over and over again and those are the people you should be working with.

CHAPTER 5

NO NONSENSE MISTAKES TO AVOID

In this chapter we will go over the top 10 mistakes that I see newer investors make. If I'd known what I know now when I first started, it could have saved me a lot of headaches. In other words, don't hesitate to read this chapter several times. It will be worth your while.

1. *Getting Advice From the Wrong People*
   I could probably write a whole book on why you need to be very careful about who you get advice from, but I will try to keep it shorter. If you tell people that you will start flipping houses or get started in real estate investing, they will tell you every reason under the sun why you should not.

   The only problem is the people telling you this don't want to see you succeed and are often unsuccessful themselves. Here are some specific examples of people you should not listen to.

- <u>Your local know-it-all real estate agent</u>

    Let me start by pointing out there are many great real estate agents out there that love to work with investors and understand the business. However, I think we all know at least one "know-it-all real estate agent" who does not like investing and has never been successful in investing. Every area has one or several of these agents that can give you every reason why house flipping does not work.

    The only problem is, they have never done a successful deal. In fact, they often tried house flipping at one point in their career and failed miserably. As a result, they still have a bad taste in their mouth. Stay away from these people and take everything they say with a grain of salt.

- <u>CNN or Fox News headlines</u>

    It seems like every week there is a new stat or dramatic headline about house flipping, usually on one of the big news networks. Sometimes they say house flipping is back, and sometimes house flipping is dead. Either way, the news is often reported by someone who is not a full-time house flipper and really has no idea what they are talking about.

At any point in the economy you could cherry-pick various stats that could make it seem like house flipping is back or house flipping is dead. Stats lie and can be manipulated to support any argument, so try to stay away from those dramatic clickbait headlines you might see on the news or online.

- <u>Friends and family members</u>
This one is harder because friends or family members can have a negative outlook on house flipping. They may say it's too risky, they may say it's a scam, they will ask you why you don't just work a normal, steady job with a consistent paycheck. I've heard all of these. When you get into this business, you have to think about your goals and stay focused. Don't listen to people who try to discourage you from becoming an investor.

To reiterate this point, here are examples of people you *should* listen to.

- <u>Successful investors that are interviewed on podcasts, YouTube, and elsewhere</u>

  These days there are tons of great podcasts out there that interview successful investors from across the country doing different types of deals in different types of markets. Some of the podcasts include *BiggerPockets, Best Ever Show, Epic Real Estate*, and many more.

  All of these people are full-time real estate investors who worked other jobs before making the jump into real estate investing. You can learn a lot from their stories and theirs trials and tribulations.

- <u>Full-time house flippers that you meet at REIA meetings or in Meetup groups</u>

  The person running your local REIA or various people you may meet at one of these real estate investing associations are often full-time house flippers. They can share insights and in some cases even offer different opportunities to work together and partner with local investors getting started.

  A full-time real estate investor that you meet

in a REIA or Meetup group, especially a local one, will have a very different opinion on real estate investing than a CNN headline or a jaded real estate agent. I can guarantee it.

- <u>Coaching or mentoring programs</u>
  When I first got started in real estate investing, I joined a coaching program. Although it was expensive, it was one of the best decisions I've ever made. There is a whole world of real estate investing and house flipping that 99% of the population does not even know about.

  Gaining this specialized info from a coaching program put me much further ahead of the competition. The people who start these programs have often done hundreds, if not thousands, of real estate deals and are the best at what they do.

2. *Getting in Over Your Head*
   I have talked to literally hundreds if not thousands of newer investors who have never flipped a house before. Occasionally they will ask me about a lead they are working on that involves knocking down

a house and subdividing three lots or building a new construction. My first response is, "Why in the world would you want to do that as your first deal?" Building a house, much less subdividing a property, is something that even some developers who have been in the business for over ten years don't do.

Unless you come from a construction background, when you are getting started with your first deal, I would recommend choosing a simpler project, i.e. a house that just needs cosmetic work or just wholesaling a deal to a more experienced investor.

The thing with investing is that projects almost always cost more and take longer than anticipated. That is why you need to start small with something manageable. Townhouses, condos, or small single-family houses work great for your first deal. Stay away from properties that need large additions, new construction, or complete gut jobs.

3. *Weird Houses*

Sometimes investors want to get my opinion on deals they are looking at, but then they send me what I consider "weird houses". Weird houses to me are houses that fit a couple of different requirements. For starters, they may be unusually small for the neighborhood and, therefore, unusually low-priced.

While it may look like a good deal if a house is unusually small for the area, I need to see at least a couple of sold houses that are of the same size. Just because the price is significantly lower does not mean it's a good deal. A house that small will take a lot longer to sell and will sell for a lot less than the neighborhood.

Another characteristic of weird houses is teardowns. You can come across these uninhabitable teardown houses in many neighborhoods, and you should be careful because they will sell for significantly less than other homes and could skew your comps.

The best way to get a good idea of what these teardowns are worth is to look at any new construction homes in your area and what price the builder paid for the house by searching the tax records or Zillow.

You should see a trend of what builders pay for teardown houses in your area. If you are still unsure, then you can ask a more experienced investor and possibly partner on the deal.

Anytime I come across a deal that is over my head I present the deal to a trustworthy and more experienced partner who lets me know what I should do with it. Usually, we end up splitting it or getting an assignment fee.

Lastly, the third characteristic of weird houses is that they are often located right on a busy road or in front of a large landmark, like a school. I try to avoid houses on busy roads and in front of schools, gas stations, fire stations, or any type of large landmark besides a park. While there are certainly exceptions, you need to factor in a much lower price for houses on busy roads and only use comps that sold on that busy road.

Houses just one block away on a quieter street have a very different value. Whatever you do, make sure not to buy a house on a busy road, in front of a school, in teardown condition unless you have a lot of experience.

4. *Partnering With the Wrong People*

    For your first couple of deals, I would recommend doing the deal just by yourself or with a more experienced full-time investor. The likelihood of deals going bad is higher when you're new to the game, so I would avoid working with friends or family until you have more experience. When you are first getting started, it is very tempting to partner with everyone on your deal.

    However, I would be very careful about it, especially with your first deal. The bottom line is: never jump into any business relationship full-time until you have some experience. Start with smaller projects, and then scale up the business and partnership if you see fit. There can be amazing relationships and not so amazing ones, so always start small, and make sure the person has a good reputation and that you know them well.

5. *Not Evaluating Enough Deals*

    People often ask me what I think about a house right next door to them. They think it's a deal just because it's for sale, or maybe it looks vacant and appears to be a good prospect for a flip. I always tell new investors that they should see at least 100 houses before they buy their first flip.

Now, you don't necessarily need to drive to 100 houses and go inside each one, but run 100 different houses through your deal analyzer so that you have an idea of what price point a good deal is. Keep in mind that most houses are not good deals. Just because your neighbor's house is for sale does not mean it is a good flip opportunity. As an investor, you really have to qualify and cherry-pick the best deals.

6. *Overpaying for Houses*

    Newer buyers often assume they would make a profit if they bought a house at 200K and sell it for 300K. While that could be true, you need a better formula than that. You need to have a deal analyzer, which you can get by downloading from my website. A deal analyzer qualifies the deal and shows you exactly how much you could make on it, taking into account holding costs, commissions, and repair costs, and using a conservative after repair value or ARV.

    Another way to quickly tell if it's a good deal or not is using the MAO formula, or maximum allowable offer, which states that your maximum allowable offer should be the after repair value times .7 minus the cost of repairs. We have a whole chapter on evaluating deals, but you need to use the MAO formula on all deals.

Lastly, if you don't have a deal analyzer and you don't use the MAO formula, at the very least there should be a big difference between what you are paying for the house and what the Zillow value is. For example, these are the last two houses I bought: for one house, the Zillow value was 240K, and I bought it for 115K. The other house's Zillow value was 625K, and I bought it for 350K.

7. *Not Following a Proven Formula*

Take marketing for deals as an example. I always recommend the tried-and-true marketing strategies of direct mail, bandit signs, cold calling, MLS searches, strategic networking, car magnets, and online marketing for investors who are just getting started. Choose one, get a couple of leads, and then grow it from there. However, you would not believe how many people will try some pie-in-the-sky marketing strategy that I've never heard of.

One investor I recently consulted with told me he had paid a grocery store for thousands of ads on grocery carts. Now, while I am always to open to trying new marketing strategies, why would you ever try something like that as your first marketing campaign?

Last time I checked, there were not thousands of articles and trainings on how to market correctly at grocery stores, and probably for a good reason. Stick with the proven strategies first, and then venture onto the other types.

8. *Expecting the Market to Increase*
   When you are buying houses, you need to assume that the market will stay where it is currently at. If properties have sold for 200K renovated over the past year, then that is the number you need to use in your analysis. You should not factor in any type of increase in sales price because you think the market will go up.

   With flipping, you never buy for appreciation. If it happens, then that's a bonus, but never factor it into your equation. That is how a lot of people got in trouble with the market crash of 2008: they just assumed that property values would keep inflating, until it was too late.

9. *Not Evaluating Repairs Correctly*

    With real estate investing it is best to systematize everything. When it comes down to evaluating repairs, that is no different. You need a repair estimator (which you can get on my website) that can give you a good estimate of what repairs cost.

Depending on where you live, repairs will be different, so you need a couple strategies to decide repair costs. For starters, there is a free website called HomeAdvisor.com, which can tell you exactly what it costs based on your zip code for different home repairs. It even gives you a low estimate, a medium estimate, and a high estimate for different repairs.

Next, you should be talking to other real estate investors and looking at as many case studies as you can about what they are paying to renovate properties. You can do that at local REIAs and Meetup groups.

The key to a repair estimate is not to be 100%

accurate but to be in the ballpark. If you think a house needs 25K worth of work, but it really needs 50K, then your budget will be completely screwed up. With the repair estimator I use, I put in all the repairs, and it automatically adds 10% to any repair budget, just to be conservative. That will make your evaluations much more accurate.

10. *Focusing on Too Many Exit Strategies*

When you are getting started, you should already have in mind what you are looking to do – whether that is rehabbing it, wholesaling, or buying and holding. Your exit strategy will determine how you go about finding properties.

For example, if you are looking to rehab, then you should look on the MLS, do direct marketing, networking, and online advertising. However, if you are only wholesaling, for example, then should only be looking at off market properties from leads that you generate, (i.e. do not look on the MLS for wholesale deals).

Choose your strategy, get a couple of deals done that way, and then expand on your exit strategies. Like I've said before, most of the best investors will have several different exit strategies. At any given time they may be working on a couple of rehabs, wholesaling a deal, and own several rental properties that generate cash flow every month.

CHAPTER 6

STRATEGIES TO FUND YOUR DEAL

Funding your deal is the most important part of real estate investing if you are doing a rehab. Fortunately, there are several ways to get funding, even if you don't have any money yourself.

The first way is something a lot of real estate investors use: hard money. Hard money is short-term loans for investors that charge anywhere from 12 to 15% and 2-5 points. Although it sounds expensive, a good hard money lender can typically fund your deal in as little as a week or ten days.

The reason real estate investors pay more for this type of money is that it is fast and flexible. In most scenarios, a hard money lender funds 65% ARV, which means that, even with the best deals, you still have to bring some money to the table, usually at least 10%. However, many investors I know have another friend or associate who provides those funds.

We talk about how to find the best hard money lenders in another chapter; however, keep in mind that each hard money lender will offer different rates and have different ways of doing business, so it's important to reach out to several of them to get an idea.

Partnering is another option, but it is the most expensive one. Nevertheless, many people do this when they are getting started since they don't have the track record yet. Partnering is exactly what it sounds like: you find a partner — maybe a friend or real estate associate — who has the money and you decide on what your partnership should be. Sometimes it is 50/50, and sometimes it might be 60/40. It is completely up to you and what you think is fair.

Usually, one person will find and manage the deal, while the other person will fund it and possibly take more risk. After doing a deal or two this way, ideally, you would want to evolve to a less expensive type of funding, such as hard money, and eventually private money.

Private money is the least expensive and most flexible form of funding. This is what your eventual goal should be: to have enough private lenders so that you can have as many projects as you can handle every month. Private money works like this: your investor will completely or partially fund your deal and rehab costs.

They are essentially the bank, and in exchange for borrowing the money, you will sign a promissory note and a mortgage note that secures their funds to the property. Private money is a great alternative to a traditional bank, which can take forever, as well as hard money, which can be much more expensive.

The best thing about private money is that it is completely negotiable for you and your investor. I see many private money loans at around 10-12% with zero points, as opposed to the 12-15% and two to five points you might see with hard money. The way you find private money lenders is by building relationships with other real estate professionals and other professionals. Your private money lenders might often come through referrals from other investors, agents, or even friends and family.

Your end goal should be to build up a roster of private money lenders that you can draw from at any time instead of just relying on one or two. Often, once you have done one successful deal with a private money lender, they will be lining up to do a second deal with you and tell everyone they know about it.

Conventional financing is the most common way to go when you are purchasing a property. In some cases you can even finance your first flip this way. Banks are a lot more strict than a hard money lender or private money lender, so if you are looking to finance your first flip with a conventional loan, then the property cannot be in too bad a shape. However, you can find plenty of homes that are in original condition and just need some sprucing up.

Banks typically won't loan conventional financing on properties that need extensive work, such as homes that have roof leaks and foundation issues, for example. In general, all major systems, such as HVAC, electrical, and plumbing, need to be in working condition.

Buying a fixer upper with conventional financing can be a great way to get started, and you could even live in the property and rent out a room or two to pay for some of the upgrades and save money.

In this chapter we covered several different ways of financing your first flip, including hard money, private money, partnerships, and conventional financing. You should be familiar with all of these ways of financing because they all have their time and place in the real estate investing world.

I know plenty of investors who may have one deal going with hard money, one with private money, and possibly even a partnership going – all at the same time. Do what works for you when you are getting started. Your long-term goal should be to use a combination of mostly private money (the least expensive) and hard money (the most flexible).

CHAPTER 7

SAVVY WAYS TO BUILD YOUR TEAM

When you are starting out in real estate investing, you need to think of your business as a team, as if you are creating the Dream Team of real estate investing. Some of the major players on your team should include real estate agents, wholesalers, contractors, title companies, and hard money lenders. You will also add other people to your team, and I would recommend keeping everyone in a database, or at the very least, an Excel spreadsheet.

Finding Title Companies

Finding a good title company is a lot easier than it used to be. If you've never bought a house before, a title company is where you go to sign the paperwork to purchase or sell the home. Thanks to the market crash of 2008, a lot of the bad apples were weeded out, including some title companies. Nowadays, the process of closing is very regulated, and companies that are not performing will be out of business.

The best place to find an investor-friendly title company is through referrals from other investors and real estate agents. You can call and ask title companies if they are investor-friendly, like I did when I was getting started. However, I can assure you they will say yes regardless of whether or not they work with a lot of investors, since they don't want to turn down business. It's best to get a couple of referrals for title companies and try out several before deciding on which one you want to use.

Keep in mind as well that other investors do not mind sharing this resource with you. In some cases, they might even get discounts on their future deals by referring as many people as possible. So be sure to ask as many real estate professionals as possible about their preferred title companies, because you will start to hear some of the same names over and over again. Those names are the people you want to work with.

Finding Hard Money Lenders

Having a good hard money lender on your team can be the difference between getting deals done and not.

A hard money lender is the person that will lend you the majority of the money for your flip deal, so you need them to be responsive and easy to work with. It is very important that you find a couple of highly reputable hard money lenders that have been in business for a while and have good reviews.

When getting started, keep in mind that every city has anywhere from 10 to 100 hard money lenders operating in that area. Each hard money lender has a slightly different way of doing business and will charge you different amounts as well. Usually, once you have done a deal or two with a hard money lender, they will lower their rates.

The first deal is usually the highest rate: somewhere in the range of 15% and two to five points on your money. Some hard money lenders even offer joint venture opportunities or might be willing to wholesale your deal since they have such a huge buyers list.

The best way to find hard money lenders is first doing an online search of hard money lenders in your city. After building a list of 10-20, you should start looking at their reviews and checking out their websites. Just from doing that, you should be able to tell who is more legitimate than others. You can then reach out and talk to them about how they work, and let them know you are a newer investor looking to build a long-term relationship.

You should also be networking at REIAs and real estate Meetup groups, where other investors will tell you who they prefer over others. Sometimes the REIAs or Meetup groups are sponsored by hard money lenders so that is another way to find them. You ideally want to have at least three solid hard money lenders that you trust and that get good reviews or come recommended.

Finding Wholesalers

Wholesalers can be a beneficial and important part of your real estate investing team. The reason is that they will essentially bring you off-market real estate opportunities for free. The key to working with wholesalers when you are getting started is to have a lot of them on your team. By "team" I simply mean a list on an Excel spreadsheet or a database where you have their name, number, and any other information you care to input.

You do not want to rely on just one wholesaler because wholesalers will often send you so-so deals or will not properly evaluate the repair budget.

You build up your list of wholesalers by going to REIA meetings and Meetup groups, writing down any number you see on bandit signs, and going on LinkedIn, typing in "wholesaler", and then going to your city. For each city there should be a list of at least ten or 25. If you eventually build up a list of 20 or even 50 wholesalers, then you can start to see tons of off-market leads and potentially buy one of them. I would look at wholesaler leads the same way you might look at any other lead: most are not good, but one or two in ten might have potential.

Finding Agents

When you first get started in real estate investing, I would recommend finding out who the investor-friendly agents in your area are. Eventually, you want to get your own license because it is not only surprisingly easy to get licensed, but it can also save you money down the road, since you can list your own properties or refer listings and buyers to full-time agents.

The best place to find investor-friendly agents is at local REIA and Meetup groups. You can also search online on websites like LinkedIn, where you can just type in "real estate agent" and click on your city. You should have several hundred agents show up, and then you can go through their profiles, see who would work with investors, and reach out.

Also, everyone knows a friend or cousin who just got their license and can set you up on an automatic search for properties that need work. Tell them to set you up on a search for properties that meet certain keywords in the descriptions, such as "as is", "handyman special", "investors", "cash only", and other keywords.

I would not recommend signing any type of buyer agent agreement with a real estate agent because you are an investor. The investment deal could come from anywhere or anyone, so you don't want to be tied to one person. Any agent that does not understand that is someone you probably should not work with. Keep in mind that most agents do not work with investors, so you may have to go through five or ten agents to find an investor-friendly one.

Finding Contractors

When you are getting started as a real estate investor, finding a good contractor is of major importance. In this chapter we will go over three quick strategies that work in finding the best contractors.

Tip number one: Get a referral for a contractor from somebody in the business or someone that just had work done on their house. You can ask real estate agents, other investors, friends, or anybody you trust – ideally, someone in real estate. Most people don't have any issue whatsoever with recommending a contractor. It's even better if you can get a couple of referrals on contractors and then meet with three of them at a potential house you are looking at to see who would do the best job.

Always do an online check of the contractor as well. Just because they are referred does not guarantee anything, although it does weed out a lot of bad contractors. Look online to make sure the contractor does not have bad reviews, and always make sure they have a license and insurance.

Tip number two: Go to the top real estate agent

websites in your area and browse around. Typically, the top real estate agents will have a section on their website called "recommended vendors" or "recommended contractors".

This is a gold mine, and you can build a substantial list of vetted contractors by going to a couple of these agents' sites. Once you have several names, you can cross-reference them with an online search of ratings/reviews to make sure they have a license and are insured.

Tip number three: Anytime you are driving around and see a house being renovated, you'll typically see a sign out front advertising their business (i.e. Bill's contractor services). Write down their name and number, or even take a photo of their sign so that you can add it to your list of contractors. You generally only want to hire "busy" contractors, since there is usually a reason they are busy. You should be wary of contractors that are not actively doing work.

By using these three strategies, you should be able to build up a large list of already vetted contractors in your area. Keep in mind too that some contractors will do a great job for a couple of projects and then start slacking off on the next ones, so that's why you always want to have several options. Also, I would always recommend starting on a smaller project first with your rehab deal. If it works out with that contractor, then consider doing larger projects.

CHAPTER 8

ADVICE FOR SELLING YOUR FIRST DEAL

I want to give you some strategies that would have saved me a lot of time and energy for when you sell your first deal. When starting out, you should do three things that will ensure a successful sale if you decide to do a rehab.

To start with, find a local reputable real estate agent who gets great reviews online and comes highly referred from a friend or another investor. You want to have a local agent who specializes in that area and has sold houses in that area before. I see people that try to either list the property themselves or just use an MLS placement service for which they might pay just $500 or so.

I would advise against this because the property will sit on the market for months on end, the listing will become stale, and then you will start getting a lot of lowball offers. It's best to go with a professional who can get the job done from the start. They will be able to price the property correctly and make sure that it sells in a timely manner.

Secondly, make sure the real estate agent uses a professional photographer for their real estate listings. You want your property to be as presentable as possible, so make sure the agent is not just taking photos of the house on their phone. These days everybody starts their real estate searches online. If your photos are not professionally done, buyers will ignore your property and move on to the next one.

Lastly, I would recommend staging. Most people cannot envision how a property will look with furniture in it and think that rooms are much smaller than they are. Vacant houses can often seem cold and uninviting, so by having a good stager, you can warm your property up and make it much more presentable. About five years ago we never staged properties, but then we tried it a couple times and realized how much faster properties sell with good staging. Now we do it for nearly every property.

When it comes to rehabbing a house, If you have a good real estate agent who knows the market and lists your house at the correct price, professional photography, and a professional stager, the likelihood of your house selling quickly at a good price will be significantly higher.

CONCLUSION

IT'S YOUR TURN TO FLIP

After reading this book, you should have everything you need to start your first flip.

I purposely made this book short and straight to the point. I would even recommend reading it twice so you can internalize everything we have talked about here. If you follow the steps in this book, you will be ahead of 99% of the competition looking to get into flipping.

I wrote this book because I wanted to share the steps involved in your very first flip and explain what you need to know about real estate investing if you have never flipped before. It is an interesting and unique niche of business that can be mastered, just like any other skill.

There are full-time real estate investors in every market. By following the blueprint I have laid out, there is no reason why you cannot achieve that status sooner rather than later.

The first step is to take action, start marketing, and look for deals. Focus on one of the strategies we talked about – whether that's MLS searches, direct mail, bandit signs, car magnets, networking, or online marketing and just start generating leads. If there was one thing I could tell myself looking back to when I got started, it would be to become a lead generation master. If your phone is constantly ringing with sellers, you will always have opportunities to flip, even if you don't know a ton about real estate like I did when I was getting started.

There are countless examples of people who used to work full-time jobs that were not fulfilling. Through hard work, education, and taking action, they became successful full-time house flippers. By combining action-taking and consistently learning about the business, there is no way you cannot succeed.

I created this book so that you could successfully flip your first home, and then evolve beyond that into doing a couple of deals per year to eventually doing a couple of deals per month. The great thing about real estate investing is that with every deal you do, small or large, you become incrementally better and better.

It is now your turn to flip.

Thank you for getting my book! I really appreciate any feedback and would love to hear your opinion. If you enjoyed this book, please leave me a helpful review on Amazon.

Thank you!

BONUS CHAPTER

HOUSE-FLIPPING HACKS FOR NEW INVESTORS

I just wanted to throw in a list of the best house flipping hacks for new real estate investors that I could think of. We have already touched upon a couple of these, but I wanted you to have them in a list format so that you could refer to them when necessary.

1. For wholesaling your first deal, you can partner with more experienced investors. The top wholesalers in your area typically have thousands of people on their buyer lists. You can do a so-called "co-wholesale": they will send your deal out on their list to thousands of potential investors, and then you will split the deal.

    It's a great way to get your first deal done, since they will do most of the work, and you just have to find the good leads.

2. One of the best places to find good contractors is by browsing different local real estate agents'

websites. They typically have a section on their site called "preferred vendors". You can start building a list of contractors from there and then cross-reference them with online reviews.

3. When you are not sure if a deal is good, the fastest way to tell is this. Go on Zillow and look at the Zestimate. There typically needs to be a big difference between the Zestimate and what the seller is looking to sell the house for.

   As an example, for the last two houses I bought, the Zestimate was about double of what I bought the property for. It doesn't always have to be that extreme, but if you think you might have a deal, always run it by another investor that you trust.

4. The best way to handle all the leads you get is a call-answering service. It is much less expensive than hiring an acquisitions person and will save you lots of time. For just a couple of hundred bucks a month you can have a full-time answering service, such as AnswerFirst or PAT Live, screening calls for you and sending you a text or email anytime you get a lead.

   The top investors all use these types of services.

They are easy to set up, you just give them a lead interview script where you ask the seller basic property info such as address, condition of house, and what price they are looking for.

5. You should listen to as many interviews of successful real estate investors as possible. The best way to do that is through freely available podcasts, such as Bigger Pockets, Best Ever Show, Epic Real Estate, and many others. There are plenty of apps, such as Stitcher, that you can download and listen to on 2X speed.

In just one hour, you can probably listen to several investors' journeys to becoming an investor, the marketing strategies they use, as well as numerous other helpful tips.

6. If you are looking to build a list of real estate investors in your area for your buyers list or for research purposes, the most effective way is using LinkedIn. You can go on there, type in "real estate investor", and then click on your city.

If you live in a large city, there should be hundreds of people that show up on that list. You can connect with them, or at least get their contact info, and start building your database.

7. If you have repetitive tasks that you would prefer to not do, then use a service such as Fiverr or Upwork. You can have a virtual assistant do various tasks for $5 or less an hour. This can be a great resource for things like building a list, researching properties, online marketing, and much more.

8. Learn the zoning laws of your area. This is a somewhat more advanced strategy, but most people in the real estate industry — including agents and other investors — have no idea about the zoning laws. If you spend some time reading the publicly available zoning laws from your county and city, you will start to see deals where others do not.

   I know that from first-hand experience: I sold a house that could have been converted into a five-unit condo building, and I lost out on a huge payday as a result of that. Then I became an expert!

9. If you can generate 25-50 leads a month, then you can be a full-time house flipper in any market.

You need 25-50 leads because most leads are not motivated sellers, but one or two in ten leads will have potential. By 25-50 leads a month, I mean people calling you directly from your direct mail, online marketing, or wholesalers bringing you off-market deals. The best way to get to 25-50 leads a month is to start by getting your first lead, then make it a goal to get ten leads a month, then 20, and you are on your way.

10. The most effective way to generate leads for your first flip — or any flip, for that matter — is direct mail. I personally use a service called www.click2mail.com to send out my mail, although there are probably hundreds of mail services out there. If you have never done a direct mail campaign, don't worry — you can use the exact same postcard that I use by going to my website and downloading a copy for free.

Want More Training?

Go to **www.jeff-leighton.com** for helpful videos, free resources, downloads, additional mentoring, online programs, and much, much more. You can also text **DEAL to 345345** to stay updated on everything we have going on in the real estate investing world.

Other Books By The Author

Available on Amazon

Follow Jeff Leighton

Instagram.com/JeffRLeighton
YouTube.com/JeffLeighton1
Facebook.com/JeffLeighton5

PROBATE REAL ESTATE INVESTING

The Ultimate Guide to Buying and Selling Probate Real Estate

PREFACE

Dear Friend,

Welcome to Probate Real Estate Investing, The Ultimate Guide To Buying and Selling Probate Real Estate. This book represents years of hard work, experience, and marketing tests to give you only the best strategies that work onto find deals on a consistent basis.

I wanted to take a moment and let you know what to expect from this book.

First of all, this is not a theoretical fictional book. These strategies and stories are all from direct experience in the world of probate real estate investing. I do not have a PHD in real estate from a prestigious university and I will not be able to give you 100 different theories on the real estate market.

What I do have is practical experience from doing numerous deals and continuing to do deals to this day. There will also be opportunities throughout the book to go deeper in the content and gain access to additional real world probate content in the form of training videos, classes, and any inevitable updates I will be making to the book.

Second, this is a business book for implementers. The way this book is set up there are going to be practical action items in every chapter so you know exactly what to do in setting up a probate real estate machine in your area. You will get tons of ideas that you can use to grow or start your real estate business in this unique niche.

Third, this book was not created to be a NY Times Bestseller or win any awards for writing. While I could have easily made this book 50,000 words and hired a team of editors I decided that this book would be a straight to the point, real estate investing guide, that was created to help you to start doing these deals as soon as possible. There is not a lot of fluff in this book, we dive right in to the good stuff when it comes to finding probate deals.

Having said all that, if you like what you read from the book, or at least the majority of it I would absolutely love to hear from you and find out more about you. My contact information and social media profiles are at the end of this book and I would love to connect with you or answer any of your questions you may have.

I hope this guide helps you save time and money, and gets you to start doing probate deals ASAP!

CHAPTER 1

WHAT YOU NEED TO KNOW ABOUT PROBATE

The probate industry is a little-known yet highly lucrative trillion-dollar industry that, once mastered, can be a steady source of business.

So how does probate work, and what is it exactly?

The probate process varies in each state. I am not a lawyer, so we will not get into the nitty-gritty. However, you don't need all the information anyways. You just need to know the basic steps of the process, since you typically will not have much interaction with any court or lawyer.

In a nutshell, probate is the legal process which happens after someone passes away. It involves the transfer of property to the rightful heirs or beneficiaries and paying off any debts from the estate.

This is what you need to know: when you get a

probate list or find a probate file, you will have access to the Personal Representative's or Executor's contact information - and that is what you are looking for. Once their name appears in the courthouse records, it means they have been appointed by the courts to make a decision regarding the property in the estate.

In the majority of cases, they are looking to sell. Often, the executor might be a relative, friend, associate, or even a lawyer. They usually have a motivation to sell the property sooner rather than later in the most hassle-free way possible. That is where you, as the investor, come in and make them an offer. We will go over exactly how to market to these people in a later chapter; however, I have found them to be very responsive and motivated.

I believe this is a great niche for a couple of reasons. Number one, there is less competition than in foreclosure. Most people who get started in real estate investing head straight to the foreclosure properties, but they can be overrun with competition.

The great thing about probate is that, even though some people know about it, there are very few who actually market to these people, and even fewer who do it well. That leaves a huge opportunity to a savvy, consistent, and patient marketer.

Another reason why it is a great niche is that it is a trillion-dollar industry. From my own research and experience I have found that the overwhelming majority of people in probate sell their house within a year. I can almost guarantee you that you won't be able to find another group of sellers in the general population more motivated than that. Marketing is all about aiming your message at the right prospects - and this is about as motivated as they come.

These sellers typically inherit properties that need a good amount of work. They might also have several heirs that are looking to get paid out as soon as possible. That creates a great amount of motivation to get the property sold in the most efficient manner possible (i.e. not using a real estate agent). Hence, you can add value by offering the seller a fair, as is, no-real estate agent-commissions offer with a fast close.

It allows you to get a great deal and the seller to sell exactly how they want - easily - and to get the property off of their back. Usually, the house is completely paid off (unlike foreclosures) and vacant, which makes it easier to do estimates and close the deal.

Keep in mind that, with probate, you really only need to do one or two good deals a year to make a significant income. If you have a good marketing system set up, you will be able to find these types of deals in any market, no matter how competitive.

When I did my very first probate deal, I knew basically nothing about how it worked in a highly competitive market. People were telling me I shouldn't even try - and I made 35K without even swinging a hammer.

I would recommend reading as much as you can about the probate process in your area, but also keeping in mind the most important thing. As soon as you see someone's name published as the Executor or Personal Rep, it usually means they can sell the property. When a seller asks me a question about probate, my response is almost always the same. I am not a lawyer and not giving you legal advice; however, in my experience, once you are the PR, you are allowed to make a decision about selling or not.

I have done probate deals in three different states and used the same line for each one, which has worked successfully. Sometimes the courthouse in your area might even have a short guide in which you can learn the exact ins and outs of your county.

CHAPTER 2

MISCONCEPTIONS ABOUT PROBATE

The probate industry is riddled with misconceptions that can scare a lot of would-be investors or real estate agents away. In this chapter, I will address the top misconceptions I come across. Keep in mind that many people in the real estate industry - and in general - will have an opinion on something they really know nothing about. You should only listen to people with experience. If you listen to advice from someone who has never done a probate deal, then there are some serious issues with both you and the other person.

Length of time

Many people think the probate process can take over a year to complete. While the entire probate process can certainly take that long, the most important part (selling the property) can happen as soon as the executor is appointed. Any time you get a probate list, that is the only piece of information you are really looking for.

As long as you have the executor, you can rest assured they can now make the decision to sell - and they often do, quickly. The longest probate deal I ever did took me six months; however, it was because there were tenant issues with the property. It had nothing to do with the probate process itself.

Probate is not like doing a short sale. Often, you can get a response from the seller (personal representative) within a day or so. They are almost always looking to sell as soon as possible, usually within a month. If it makes you feel better, if other investors in your area ask about probate, tell them the process can take over a year (which is technically true). That will probably scare them away.

What you are doing is illegal or unethical

My thoughts on investing in probate are as follows. In the majority of cases, you have a seller who just inherited a property that has not been updated in original condition, is racking up fees (taxes, etc.), and is sitting vacant. The seller who is representing an estate often wants to sell as soon as possible so that they can get their share of the estate.

They have absolutely no interest in putting the property on the market, signing a 30-page real estate listing contract, and then putting it on the market with a real estate agent, hoping it might sell in a month or six.

They want the easiest, fastest offer possible and are willing to give a good deal to an investor who can provide them with that. You, as the investor, are often taking a bit of a risk by purchasing a home in original condition. For that risk, and the ease of the transaction, you get a pretty good deal in most cases.

The bottom line is, the seller is not looking to squeeze out every penny from these types of sales, and you, as the purchaser, can help them sell quickly and easily for a win-win transaction.

You need to have a specialized knowledge and lots of experience to do probate deals

When I first got started with several deals, I literally had no idea what I was doing besides mailing to the executor of properties and making them offers. I did not know special terms like beneficiaries of trust, etc.

Many technical aspects of the probate niche are still unfamiliar to me. I rely on my title company and/or the probate courts to answer questions I don't know the answer to. Sellers typically don't ask too many technical questions. If they do, I refer them to the proper sources. All I give them is my offer.

Once we're signed up, I get that paperwork over to my title company. While I would recommend that you learn as much as you can, I would not let lack of knowledge with probate stop you from getting started and making offers.

Everybody markets to probate, so there is no more opportunity

First of all, that's just not true. While many people may say they market to probate or have tried marketing to probate, what they really mean is, they may have sent out 25 letters one time to a probate list. After not receiving any calls, or maybe even getting a call, they heard someone else also say they market to probate, and then they came to the conclusion that the market is too saturated. In reality, you need a consistent, sharp, marketing program that includes follow-up over the course of six months, which I will show you how to do.

In every market there is always room for a good marketer, no matter how much competition there is. You could give the overwhelming majority of people an exact blueprint, a step-by-step process to do a probate deal, and they will either not do it all or make such a minimal effort that it can't have a chance of ever working.

The bottom line is, you don't need to be a probate expert; you just need to take action and start making offers. Getting leads solves all issues, as the wise Gary Keller once said. If you can consistently get 25 probate leads a month, you should be able to do deals. Don't worry about what anyone else is doing. Just focus on your own lead generation efforts, and you will get there.

CHAPTER 3

HOW TO FIND PROBATE PROPERTIES

When looking for probate properties, there are many ways you can obtain the list - some more effective than others. I have tried every way possible, and in this chapter, I will go over the most effective ways. Also keep in mind that the probate data is public information, so I would almost guarantee that your county or city has the data.

You just have to be creative in your ways to find it. If you think your city does not have the list, all you have to do is pay me enough. I guarantee I will get it for you (only half joking).

Purchasing a List

In many counties, there might be a local list provider of probate names on a weekly or monthly basis. US Probate Leads is one such provider. You might also meet someone at a local REIA meeting, or even down at the courthouse, that provides these leads to investors and real estate agents. The leads might be a little more expensive than what you are used to (think $1 to $3 per lead). However, it can also save you time, since you don't have to source the list yourself.

For beginners, I think this is certainly a good way to get started. You also want to make sure your list provider has a good reputation. You can even check their work for the first week or two by going to the courthouse yourself or checking online. I tried out a local person for a little while before eventually training someone to go down to the courthouse themselves, and they turned out to be much better.

Title Companies

One title company in my area provides probate lists for different agents and investors who send them deals on a regular basis. The key to getting a title company to compile probate lists for you is that they will need to see some type of ROI on their service relatively quickly. It is much better if you can refer the title company a couple of deals first, and then ask for the probate list.

Many title companies won't have the probate list; however, some will. If they don't have the probate list for different counties, they may have other motivated sellers lists, such as pre-foreclosure, tax liens, etc. Title companies can be a great marketing resource. Some will even offer to pay for your marketing in return for sending the deals.

Going to the Courthouse Yourself

When I first got started in probate real estate investing, I would go to the courthouse myself. That was probably the most accurate way of getting the list, since I was getting it directly from the source. However, it also took up a lot of my time. Building a list is a $10/hour job, and eventually, I got smart and hired someone to build the list for me (after training them). That allowed me to use my time in a more effective way.

The process is very simple: all you have to do, is go to your local courthouse and look at the directory for the probate room. Usually, there are a couple of computers in there with instructions on how to look up the probate files for the previous weeks or months.

When you are getting started, I would recommend going down to the courthouse a few times and getting used to pulling the files so that you can get a better understanding of how it works. Some courthouses will allow you to bring a laptop in, so you can build the list on an excel spreadsheet, while others will only allow you to bring a notepad.

Either way, you are looking for the Personal Representative or Executor's mailing address and any other contact information they may have. You also want to be sure there is property associated with the probate file. Usually, it is pretty obvious whether or not there is any real estate with the file. Each probate file will only be about five to 15 pages, and there should be one sheet that specifically mentions if there is property.

Once you do it a couple of times, it becomes very easy. Keep in mind, for whatever reason, I have found the people that work at the probate office to be exceptionally unhelpful. Now, it may be because people ask them for the list all the time, or maybe they don't like their jobs - I'm not sure. Either way, do not be discouraged if they tell you there is no list, they will not help you find the list, and/or any other number of excuses they will tell you.

Ninja Way - Asking Someone at the Courthouse to

Get It for You

One strategy I have tried is asking someone who works at the probate office to build this list for me. Now, keep in mind that most of the people who work at the probate office are not the highest-paid employees in the world, so they might be interested in some extra cash each week or month. You can call, go in person, or even better, if your courthouse has an online chat feature, you can message them and see if someone is interested.

Now, I haven't actually gotten somebody to do this for me yet. However, I have not tried this strategy very hard, and I think it could work if you find the right person. Remember to be persistent; one person may tell you to get lost, while another would be thrilled to get some extra cash each week or month.

Getting the Information Online

If you are a tech or computer nerd like myself, you should be able to figure out how to get the probate information online for your county. It took me a little while to figure out this strategy, but in my opinion, getting the probate data online is *by far* the best strategy. You can subscribe to your courthouse records and/or find the public records for your county online.

Once you find that data, you can hire a virtual assistant for $3 an hour to build a probate list for you for every county within an hour's drive of you. I say within an hour's drive because it's cost effective to build a list that way, and sometimes you might come across a six-figure deal that just happens to be about an hour away (ask me how I know). While I prefer to do deals right down the street, if you want to increase your deal flow, you should increase your marketing prospects.

Legal Journals/Newspapers

Another way to get the probate data is through legal journals in your area. According to my understanding of probate law, all probate cases have to be published in a newspaper, and most often they are published in legal journals. If you can find these newspapers and/or legal journals, you can have the weekly or even daily probate notices for different counties.

Most people do not know about this, but you can usually find the legal journal and/or newspaper provider in your area by doing some online research on a site called google.com. The journals that these probate notices are filed in are typically not your large newspapers like *The NY Times* or *Washington Post*.

However, you could ask the probate offices which journals publish the probate files and the clerks should be able to tell you. If not, you could always get a couple of probate files and Google their name, address, and "personal representative" or executor, and you will typically find which journal they are published in.

I have given you six different proven ways of getting probate leads. I would recommend trying all of them so that you gain an understanding of the court system. Then you can find the way that works best for you and implement a system where you can consistently get your probate marketing out on a weekly basis.

Keep in mind that each county or city is slightly different, although generally speaking, the process is the same. When I was first trying to find the list, I went to various courthouses multiple times and had numerous people tell me the lists don't exist. You have to be persistent and come at the probate list from multiple angles.

CHAPTER 4

MARKETING TO PROBATE

In this chapter, we will cover marketing, which is by far my favorite part of business. There are numerous ways to market to probate - some more effective than others. By the end of this chapter, you will have several different proven strategies for marketing to probate.

Direct Mail

I think direct mail is the best form of marketing to probate. I have done countless deals this way. It is very simple: after you get the PR, Executor, and a beneficiary or two's mailing address, you send them an email saying that you would like to purchase the property in probate.

I typically send a personalized postcard specifying the name and exact address of the probate property, saying I would like to purchase it. You do not need to get too fancy with your letter or postcard. In fact, you can just Google "probate letter or postcard", and you'll see 100 different options. If you want the actual letters and postcards that I send, just go to my website at www.jeff-leighton.com to download.

In my opinion, a personalized letter beats a generic "we buy houses" postcard or letter every day of the week. If you are sending a yellow letter or personalized letter, make sure the envelope is handwritten. If the letter looks personal, it will have a significantly higher chance of being opened and responded to.

There are many direct mail fulfillment services that will do this for you, such as Yellow Letters Complete and countless others. I also put my website, email address, 24-hour free recorded message line, and phone number on the letter or postcard, in case they would like to reach me in a different way.

You will find some seller's preferred email, text, or phone. With direct mail, I typically send one letter every 30-45 days for six months. The overwhelming majority of people will stop sending after one time, which leaves a huge opportunity for you to get these great deals that others are too lazy to market to. Many of my best deals have come after my third, or even fourth, mailer.

The key to success with direct mail is to do as many counties as you can within a reasonable radius around your area. I try to stay away from anything over an hour away. But since direct mail is so easy to send out, you may as well cover more ground. If you can cover three or four counties and be consistent with your marketing, over the course of six months or so, you can uncover some amazing deals.

Phone Call/Text

Although I do not use this strategy, I know many investors who obtain the personal representative's phone contact information from the file. Then they either call themselves or hire someone to call the executor and ask if they are looking to sell their house. This can be a very effective strategy, since it is so direct. Many sellers will tell you they are not interested, but all you need is one in a hundred to make this strategy work.

If you are too scared to call, you could also try texting the seller from a phone.com number and/or other business line. I have found sellers to be very responsive to text, and if you use a business number, they are not texting your personal cell phone. You can also use a free Google Voice phone number, which comes with texting capability. Just be sure not to send the same message to each person, or they may cancel your number (ask me how I know).

Door Knocking

An even more aggressive strategy would be door knocking and/or leaving information at the door of a personal representative or beneficiary. If you have the time and patience, this might be the best strategy, but prepare for massive amounts of rejection. Door-to-door marketing is almost always the most effective form of marketing, but it's also the most difficult to be persistent at, because you will get a ton of rejection, which most people can't handle.

Instead of just mailing the personal representative, you could leave a packet of information at the doorsteps of the executor after knocking. I know some people that even mail the executor an actual offer for the purchase of the home in probate (with an inspection of the property clause).

Overall, door knocking is the most direct way to find deals. It can also be a great way to discover neighborhoods in your area. If you don't have a ton of money or resources, you could get started by door knocking a couple of houses during your lunch break each day, or even on the weekends. If you don't feel like knocking the door, you can even just leave flyers on the door, as well as the entire block. Keep in mind that this business is all about leads, and you need at least 25 to start finding potential good deals.

Networking With Probate Attorneys

I know some investors that network with as many probate attorneys as possible and get referred many deals that way. You will realize that, just like any business, about 20 percent of the probate attorneys handle 80% of the probate cases.

Not all probate attorneys will be open to networking and lunch meetings, but really, you only need one to consistently send you deals. If you were to combine this networking strategy with a direct mail campaign, it could be very effective.

Online Marketing

As far as I know, there is no real estate investor that is yet getting consistent probate leads or deals from online marketing. However, if you are able to crack the code, please let me know so I can update this section!

After reading this chapter, you should have a lot of ideas about how to market to probate. The next step is to brainstorm what your marketing plan could be, with the idea that you can expand on it. For me, it was getting one county outsourced, then three outsourced, and eventually five. I want you to think about your marketing plan, write it down, and start implementing.

CHAPTER 5

CASE STUDIES

In this chapter, we will go over several probate case studies that have happened to me. Hopefully, you can learn from them and be prepared when they come up.

Case Study #1 - Return Calls

When I first got started, I was not the best at following up with leads as soon as I should have. I remember one specific example where I got a call over the weekend from a motivated out-of-state seller. By motivated, I mean someone that calls saying they want to sell ASAP and the house needs a lot of work. Those calls happen in about one in 10 leads that you will get. Anyway, they left a voicemail. For whatever reason, I decided I would call them back on Monday instead of right away.

By the time Monday came around, they had already had another offer. Even though I tried to offer more, they were already under contract and could not do anything. The investor got the deal of a lifetime, a significant six-figure profit, and I was left with an investing lesson. When you have a motivated seller, follow up ASAP!

Case Study #2 - Keep Things Simple

One of the biggest deals I ever made was from a seller who called me after already getting an offer. She said the first offer came from an investor who wanted to partner with her on the rehab of the home, and then they could split the profits afterwards. The investor was trying to draw up complicated joint venture paperwork with her, where she wouldn't even see a profit of the sale for at least three months.

The seller wanted no part of this house, and she especially did not want to joint venture with someone she didn't even know. She told me all she wanted was a fast close, as is, no-realtor-commission sale, which is exactly what I gave her. I kept things as simple and straightforward as possible. Because of that, I made a huge profit, while the other investor was probably left scratching his head.

The moral of the story is to keep things simple. A confused mind always says no. Let them know exactly how your offer works and don't try to complicate things.

Case Study #3 - Avoid Craigslist

During my very first wholesale deal, I made one of the biggest mistakes you could possibly make. I published my deal on Craigslist, with the exact address and all. Even though we were under contract, countless anonymous Craigslist degenerates tried to go behind my back and steal the deal from under me. "Stealing deals" almost never happens; however, if you publish a deal on Craigslist, be prepared for all types of people to go around your back.

As a result, the tenant living in the house decided they would stay several extra months, which created a huge hassle for my partner and me. The moral of the story is: use Craigslist for what it was built for, i.e. selling used furniture, getting part-time jobs, etc. Do not use it to find investors for your wholesale deals, unless you don't publish any specific information about the house. Even in that scenario, there are much better ways to find investors than Craigslist.

Case Study #4 - The Art of Following Up

Make sure the deal is 100% dead before giving up on it. For a recent deal, I received a call from a real estate agent who claimed to be representing the seller. They told me the seller had received my letter and was looking to sell their property ASAP and that it needed a lot of work.

I ran my numbers and made the offer to the agent, who abruptly stopped the call and hung up on me, not even entertaining my number. While I had been in communication with the seller a week ago, I assumed this agent was now representing them.

A couple of days later, I got a call from the seller asking me why I hadn't made my offer yet. I told her I had given her agent an offer several days ago and had been essentially told it wouldn't work. I did not realize that not only was the agent not representing the seller, but they hadn't given them my offer either.

Once I told the seller what I could offer, she immediately told me to send over the offer. We got the deal done, and it was one of the bigger deals of my career. What I learned from that was to make sure you follow up with everyone involved, especially if you are making an offer.

Case Study #5 - It's Not Just Looks That Matter

I once got a hard money loan on a probate property

that I had never seen. One of my better deals was from an out-of-state seller who was selling a condo in the perfect location within the city. It was a one-bedroom condo that needed updates. The only problem was, we would not be able to see the property until a week or so before closing. I ran all my numbers assuming that the property needed a full-gut job, and my hard money lender even agreed to fund the property without viewing the inside until the 25th hour.

I ended up buying the house. Sure enough, it needed work, but it worked out great. What I learned is that so long as the numbers work, your hard money lender may not even need to see the entire property, so long as the outside structure looks good - this was a condo, so it was not an issue.

Case Study #6 - Actions Speak Louder Than Words

Watch what people do, not what they say. There is a real estate agent in my area who goes out of his way to let it be known that he is the honest real estate agent and that probate investors are just low-ballers with no integrity. In front of clients and potential clients, he talks about why real estate investing, and the probate niche in particular, are just investors looking to lowball people and why they should not be taken seriously.

What he does not tell those same clients, but what he did tell me behind closed doors, is that when I come across these probate investment properties, to let him know first, because he would be a buyer on them. Interesting.

Now, I know it comes as a shock to you that a real estate agent might blatantly lie. However, it happens all the time. People's actions are much stronger than their words, and you must only watch what people do, not what they say. Also, since you are looking for a good deal and probate sellers are often looking for a quick and easy sale, this can be a perfect fit and a win-win situation.

These six case studies should help guide you through the probate niche. In my opinion, the best way to learn something, outside of actually doing it, is to hear stories from other investors who have gone through the steps and done deals. Hopefully these stories can save you time and money!

CHAPTER 6

COMMON PROBATE MISTAKES TO AVOID

Since I have been in this business for a while and have done a number of probate deals, I have observed exactly what you should do, as well as what you should avoid. In this chapter, we go over common mistakes people make when they do probate deals. If you want to cut years off of your learning curve, then I suggest you pay close attention to this next chapter!

Marketing One Time

I see a lot of investors struggle when they first get started for one particular reason. They typically only mail or contact the executor one time.

If there is one thing to learn from this book, it is that you should contact an executor at least three times over the course of six months - if not five times.

Sometimes the executor may not be ready to sell and forget about the letter you sent three months ago. By keeping the seller in the loop with your marketing, you can get ahead of 95% of your competition.

You don't even need to change your marketing if you don't want to. I often send the same postcard five times over the course of six to 12 months. I have had countless sellers tell me that they decided to sell to me on the third or fourth mailer.

Marketing to Every Person in Probate

In any given county, the probate files will have about 50 names a week. Out of those 50, there may only be 25 that own property. You will save yourself a lot of time, money, and headaches by mailing or marketing only to those that actually own property. If you are pulling the data yourself or hiring a virtual assistant to pull the data, it is usually very obvious whether or not there was property associated with the file. Do not market to those that don't own real estate.

Not Staying Persistent

If you want to try a probate marketing system, you need to think long term, like I briefly mentioned earlier. Plan on a six-month marketing program to test your area. If you market for just one month, you won't be able to realize the full results. If you want to see whether any direct mail campaign will be successful, you need to think long term. Also, if you set it up correctly, like the ways I go over in this book, you can put your probate marketing on auto pilot so that it only takes about 30 minutes a week and fewer resources to implement.

Listening to Unsuccessful People Talk About Probate

A lot of real estate investors, agents, or wannabe investors and agents may have an opinion on probate. If they are not currently doing probate deals, then you should take everything they say with a grain of salt. In other words, just don't listen to them. You should NOT get advice from someone not doing probate deals about doing probate deals, no matter how badly they want to tell you how it works.

Doing Everything Yourself

When I first got started, I would trek down to the courthouse myself, spend an hour there, sometimes wait by the computer for someone else to finish my research, then drive another 30 minutes to the next courthouse, and repeat the process. Although I was getting great leads, this was not the best use of my time, and it took nearly all day to get all the data.

Since then, I have saved countless hours, first by outsourcing the list building to someone I trained to get the list for me, and then, when I eventually learned how to get the data online, outsourcing to a virtual assistant. Instead of spending a whole day going through this process, I now just get the list once a week from my virtual research assistant for seven different counties!

You need to learn how to systematize and shorten the length of time it takes you to get the list. Read the short but amazing book by Michael Gerber entitled *The E-Myth,* which talks more in depth about systematizing processes like this.

This chapter covered the most common mistakes I see people make, based on my own experiences, as well as those of the hundreds of students I have consulted about their probate marketing. Keep all of them in mind when you start marketing or if you have an existing marketing plan in place.

CHAPTER 7

FREQUENTLY ASKED QUESTIONS ABOUT PROBATE

Any time I am consulting with an investor about probate, they inevitably ask me a ton of questions. Below are some of the most common questions I get. Also, with regards to the actual court process, each jurisdiction has their own policies, and they almost always have an FAQ on their website. I won't go into those specifics, since they vary by county, but they are very easy to access. Just Google "probate FAQ" and enter your county.

The main thing you need to know is that, whether it's a probate deal in Alaska, Hawaii, or Oklahoma, once the Executor has been appointed, they can sell the house. Don't get too bogged down in the other information. Keep it simple and just make offers.

Wait a second, what exactly is probate again?

All you need to know is that probate is the legal process of distributing property that is left behind when someone passes. So you contact the executor and ask them if they want to sell their house. Keep it simple. While you could read entire books on the probate specifics for each state, the main thing you need to know is that the executor or personal representative is typically looking to sell ASAP.

I did my first 10 probate deals without knowing a damn thing about the process, and I still don't know very much. Rely on the courts and/or title company to answer any other specific questions the seller may have.

Does the courthouse provide a list of names for you?

Absolutely not. They will be fairly unhelpful as well (in my own personal experience). We touched on this earlier, but you will have to build the list yourself at the courthouse. Just look on your courthouse directory, find the probate room, sit down at one of the five computers they typically have, and start pulling the data yourself while looking out only for files that have real estate.

Even though the probate clerks are typically not that helpful, I like to ask them a million questions and browse around through everything possible so that I can get a good comfort level of the courthouse and how it works. You will become an expert in no time by being nosy, asking questions, and going through as many files as possible.

Isn't there a lot of competition with probate?

There is competition with everything. I would not let a couple of other people at the courthouse worry you. You should focus on setting up a probate marketing system that can consistently generate 25 or 50 leads a month. Even if there are 1,000 other investors, as long as I can generate a steady amount of leads, it really doesn't matter what other investors do.

Some of my biggest deals have come from a seller who told me they got five other letters but just decided to call me. Also, most people that mail to probate will only do so once and will most likely only do one county. By mailing five times or so over the course of six months and doing several counties, you can be much more effective in your marketing.

Should I mail to attorneys?

I have mailed to attorneys in the past, although I typically just try to mail to the personal representative and executor. I think you could set up a strategy to network with the top probate attorneys and even mail them, but for whatever reason, it just hasn't been my thing. Attorneys can be a bit more hassle than they are worth. However, if networking or reaching out to attorneys is your thing, then by all means, you should try. In the probate business in general, you should be testing out as many things as possible to find out what works best in your specific area.

Does the person ever get mad you sent them a letter?

Every now and then, someone calls me to be taken off my mailing list. But either way, I have a call service, so I don't deal with any angry sellers. If they tell me to take them off my list, of course I will. I love getting leads and phone calls from any sellers because I know each call from a non-motivated seller is one call closer to a deal.

I also know my marketing is going out if I am getting calls. By the way, if you want a great recommendation on a call service, I use a company called Dedicated Office Systems. If you tell them I sent you, they may give me a Starbucks gift card or something, so please drop my name.

How do I make an offer on a probate house?

I make an offer on a probate house the same way I would on any other property. I use a three-page purchase and sale agreement. The only difference is that the seller might have to write "estate of..." or "personal representative of...". There is really no other big difference in making offers. This is not like a short sale where you may need a packet of information.

Once you get the contract signed, I would recommend to stay in close contact with the title company, asking if they need any additional information from the seller to make sure everyone is on the same page. Sometimes title companies may have 100 deals going on, so you need to be sure that yours is still on track to close.

When should I start marketing to probate?

I usually start marketing to probate as soon as the information of the personal representative executor becomes available in the public records. I have found that, when the information is published, it has typically been some time since the person passed away and the information is published, usually at least a month, and in some cases over a year. I have never had any issues with this, so I would recommend marketing as soon as you can.

Do the probate lawyers typically get involved?

If the seller is using a probate lawyer, which is not always the case, they typically want to get the deal done and move on. I have not had too many issues with lawyers getting involved in the real estate sale. They usually just want to see a signed contract for the purchase and sale. In most cases, that will be enough.

What is the typical response rate with probate?

It depends on what type of marketing you do, but if you are doing direct mail (which I think is by far the best), you can expect your response rate to be around 2-3%, depending on what type of mail piece you send. If it's a personalized letter, which is a little more expensive, you can get a higher response rate.

A postcard is about half as expensive, but your response rate is lower. All leads are not created equal. For example, if you get 10 or 20 probate leads, those are worth way more than 10 or 20 absentee owner leads. Probate leads are very valuable. Keep that in mind.

These are some of the most frequently asked questions I get about probate. I would recommend you read some articles about probate in your area. Just keep in mind that you do not have to be a so-called expert in probate before starting to invest. Just focus on getting leads, and then more leads.

Tracking your leads is important as well. I would recommend getting a dry erase board from Staples and putting it in a visible place. Just try to get more leads than you did the month before, until you are consistently getting 50 leads a month. I have found that to be the "golden number" where deals start coming in consistently.

CHAPTER 8

MAKING AN OFFER AND EXIT STRATEGIES FOR PROBATE

The great thing about probate properties is, since they are typically a discounted type of sale, you can have multiple exit strategies when you go to make an offer. The biggest key I would recommend is to build up as much rapport with the seller as possible, since they are usually just looking for the easiest sale from someone they know, like, and trust.

The seller's level of motivation will determine which exit strategy you should use. Also, by adding multiple exit strategies to your business, you can add more deals to your pipeline and more profit to your business at the end of the year.

Wholesale or Rehab

If they are looking for an ASAP, "as is", no-realtor-commission sale, you should try to lock the property up as soon as you can. By locking it up, I mean putting the home under contract.

Sometimes, when I put a probate property under contract, I am not sure if I will buy it myself or if I will be wholesaling it out to another investor. I have a huge list of hungry buyers, so if I get a good deal, sometimes I will let the seller know that I partner with other investors and I would like them to take a quick look at the house, usually just setting up one time to see the home. Then I will get an offer directly from the investor.

Occasionally, I might even tell the seller that this property is too high for what I am looking to purchase it at; however, I work with a lot of investors and I think one of them would be interested in the deal. If you give me a week, I can send it out to that list and let you know within seven days whether or not that price works. This can be an effective strategy to add more deals that you normally wouldn't buy to your pipeline.

Sometimes I even co-wholesale properties that I have put under contract. Then I find an investor with a massive buyer's list (think 10,000+ people). They send it out to their list, and we split the deal 50/50. If you don't have a huge buyer's list, this can be an effective strategy to wholesaling properties. You also get the advantage of having a more experienced investor work with you on the deal.

List the Property

If the seller does not need to sell ASAP and the price they are looking for is higher than what you would be willing to pay, then you can offer to list their property for them. Usually, the listing will still be an "as is" type of sale for an investor, but since you are putting it on the MLS, you could get a higher price for it.

Keep in mind that most sellers in probate just want to get rid of the property. However, you could pick up a couple of listings each year, just having this strategy in your back pocket. Most real estate agents do not market to probate. Usually, they just send out neighborhood mailers. Hence, if you are a real estate agent, a targeted mailing list like probate could be a lucrative part of your business.

Refer the Property to an Expert

If there is something unusual about a property in one of your first deals, you may be better off just referring it to a more experienced investor. Usually, they will pay you some type of finder's fee. An example of "unusual things" I have come across would be a teardown house with two lots next door to each other that the seller wants to get rid of. That scenario is a little more challenging than just evaluating a fix and flip.

Another example would be a large property in the city that could be converted into condos with the right zoning. Historic properties in high-end areas, or really anywhere, can scare a lot of investors away, but with the right person you could make a fortune off of these deals. Again, those numbers will be harder to run than most. I would try to find the big investors in your area (every city has a couple), send them over the lead, and see what they can do with it. Chances are, because of their experience, they will be able to tell you exactly if it's a deal or not.

Partner on the Deal

If there's someone you trust, you can even partner on the deal. You could set it up so that you find the deal, and they finance and fix it up. Every partnership is different. Having been in multiple partnerships, some good some bad, I would recommend a couple of things.

Make sure your partner is trustworthy and an easy person to work with. Look out for blatant red flags, such as drug addictions and lawsuits. While that may sound obvious, I have worked with partners that I should have written off from the beginning because of such issues.

If someone is using drugs, it should not matter how successful they appear on the outside; they will be a challenging person to work with. Also, if you find out someone is constantly involved in lawsuits of one form or another (I worked with a guy who told me he went to law school not to become a lawyer, but because he gets sued a lot), then you should anticipate they will be an extremely difficult person to work with.

Those are what we call "red flags". You should keep your antennas up for red flags all the time. Usually, a person's past is the best way to anticipate how they will act in the future. It's best if you partner with different people in a small capacity first to see if you are compatible, before trying to do a real estate investment deal together, since some big deals can take up to six months or even a year to complete.

Additional Things to Know About Probate

When a seller tells you the probate house is in "okay

condition", it usually means it is in original condition and will need a full rehab. Generally speaking, sellers do not like to trash their own property, although sometimes they will tell you flat out that the house needs a ton of work. Those are often the best leads because you know the seller is realistic.

If a seller does not want to tell you what price they are looking to sell their probate house for, do not be afraid to start low and work your way up. I always run my numbers using the MAO (maximum allowable offer formula), which states that your maximum allowable offer should be ARV (after renovated value) times .7 minus the cost of repairs.

When making your offer, keep things as simple as possible and give the seller what they want, a cash offer, "as is", fast close. Do not try to complicate things. Let them know they can keep anything they want in the house upon closing and do not have to fix anything.

Also, if someone is trying to give you advice on probate investing or their opinion on the probate niche, you need to think about where they are coming from. You should only get probate advice from those that have done probate deals. It is amazing to me how many unqualified people will try to give you probate advice without having done any deals.

CHAPTER 9

CLOSING THE PROBATE DEAL

Closing a probate deal in most scenarios is different than traditional types of real estate deals. This chapter focuses specifically on what you need to do to close these probate homes.

One of the most important things to getting probate deals done is finding a great title company. There are so many title companies out there, and you need one that has experience working with investors and probate homes. Your generic title company down the street that focuses 99% of their business on first-time homebuyers is not going to cut it.

In the probate world, there can sometimes be tricky issues regarding liens, beneficiaries, and more. By having an experienced title company, you can rest assured your deal will not be delayed. There are a couple of ways to find these more experienced, savvy title companies. When I first got started, I called around and would simply ask title companies if they worked a lot with investors. Almost every title company did not want to turn down business, so of course they said they did.

However, the best way to find them is to ask the experienced investors for recommendations on title companies. At any local REIA or Meetup group there will be experienced investors that would not mind sharing their title company. They may even get a discount for referring people. Either way, an experienced investor should have no issue recommending title companies.

Another GREAT source is hard money lenders in your area. Since most hard money lenders make their money doing a volume of transactions rather than just a couple, they will also know the best companies to use. Hard money lenders typically only do investment deals, and often probate transactions, so they are a great source to talk to.

If you are partnering on the probate deal or wholesaling the property to another investor, you need to make sure that investor also has experience. With probate homes, you typically might only get to see the house one time. There is usually a ton of stuff left inside the house, not to mention the homes usually need plenty of work. For a first-time, new investor or homebuyer, that can be a scary thing.

Make sure your buyer or partner is solid and won't back out upon seeing how much work needs to be done. If you have never worked with this person before, you can ask them about any other deals they may have done. At least verify their proof of funds to be sure they are legit.

In terms of what contracts you should use, that varies by state and by your own comfort level. But I would recommend keeping them as simple as possible and since I am not a lawyer you should always review any contract with an attorney.

There is one jurisdiction in my area where just getting an offer out the door requires around 45 pages, mostly filled with legal technicalities and government jargon. I instead use a three-page contract that is about as standard and simple as they come. If you want to see it, then go to my aforementioned website and download it.

The first deal I ever did was the simplest contract of

all time. It would probably not even hold up in any type of contract law. It was basically a one-page offer that included just price, date, property, and a few other minor details. The most important thing was that the seller and I were in agreement. It didn't need to be a 45-page contract covering the history of contract law and the changes in government policy over the last 50 years.

Now, I wouldn't necessarily recommend a one-page contract, but yours should be as simple as possible. If you want to, you can even run it by a lawyer, just to be sure. Usually, they will want to change it a hundred times though, so keep that in mind.

IT'S YOUR TURN TO START INVESTING IN PROBATE

Great, we have reached the end of *The Ultimate Guide to Investing in Probate Real Estate*. I hope you have enjoyed reading this book and will put it to good use. In every market, there is an opportunity to add a lucrative niche to your business. Even if it's just one deal a year, that can make a huge difference.

In this book, we have covered why you should invest in probate real estate, where to find the lists, how to market, FAQs, as well as how to close the deals. If you still have questions, I would recommend going through this book again or using it as a reference guide whenever you need it. Go step by step through what I talk about in this book, and I can guarantee you that you will see results. Having read this book, you now have everything you need to start investing in probate real estate.

Additionally, if you are looking to take your probate business to the next level and scale it up, I would encourage you to check out my online probate course that can be found at www.jeff-leighton.com.

This online program will give you in-depth information, step by step instructions, videos, and more that are impossible to include in one book.

Either way, I want to hear about any success stories you have and what you thought of the book. I hope that, when you do your first probate deal and start your probate marketing, you drop me a note and let me know that you have started.

Here's to your success!

Jeff Leighton

Want More Training?

Go to **www.jeff-leighton.com** for helpful videos, free resources, downloads, additional mentoring, online programs, and much, much more. You can also text **DEAL to 345345** to stay updated on everything we have going on in the real estate investing world.

Other Books By The Author

Available on Amazon

Follow Jeff Leighton

Instagram.com/JeffRLeighton
YouTube.com/JeffLeighton1
Facebook.com/JeffLeighton5

HOW TO ESTIMATE REPAIR COSTS ON A REHAB

A Simple System for Successful Repair Estimates as A Real Estate Investor

INTRODUCTION

Dear Friend,

Welcome to *How To Estimate Repair Costs On A Rehab*. This guide was created to make it easier for you as a real estate investor to properly estimate repairs with real numbers and no fluff. Each section gives you valuable information on evaluating repairs, including one part with actual real-life estimates that you can use today. Additionally, you can download the exact repair estimator I use in my business for free on my website.

If you are a looking for a 5-hour manual on real estate estimating with fancy diagrams and blueprints, then this is probably not for you.

However, if you are looking for a no-fluff, straight-to-the-good-stuff training on how to estimate repairs for your rehabs, then you are in the right place. This book is mostly for newer investors, although I truly believe any level of investor can gain value from this book.

When I was getting started as a real estate investor,

there was no training guide like this. I either had to buy a $50, 2000-page book on construction best practices written in contractor language or I had to search the internet and forums to find out how much different repairs cost. Neither of those were good options, so that is where this book comes into play.

Why should you listen to me? I make six figures per year as a real estate investor and have been mentored by some of the top real estate investors in the world. I'm not saying that to brag, but instead to give you an idea of where my advice is coming from.

A word of note. Because of the different prices in each respective market, I give low estimates as well as high estimates, so you will have to adjust accordingly to your area.

Moreover, this book is not for houses over a million dollars. Once you get over a million, the level of finishes, size of the rehab, and other factors can be drastically different from a house below 1 million.

This book will help you become a savvier real estate investor because you'll gain a better understanding of renovations and estimates. We will also go over how to find the best contractors, the best renovations you can do in terms of ROI, and mistakes to avoid.

I try to share stories from my own experiences throughout this book so that you can get a real-world version of it too.

I am looking forward to sharing my knowledge with you, so let's jump into it.

SECTION 1

7 THINGS YOU SHOULD KNOW ABOUT ESTIMATING REPAIRS

Before we jump into real-life estimates of all the components of a house, I want to go over seven general ideas when it comes to estimating repairs. This will help you better understand the real estate investing business and how much you should budget.

1. For starters, not every house will need a full gut renovation. You need to get a good sense of what the comps have been selling for and what condition those properties sell in.

    Sometimes the highest-selling properties are not fully renovated; they are just in good livable condition. In that scenario, it would be riskier to do a full-scale renovation and try to set a neighborhood record for price.

    Instead, you should do the sufficient repairs to bring it up to the comps, and perhaps slightly above the comps so that it stands out.

I've seen investors simply trash out the property, fix up the landscaping, and re-list the house a week or two later since the numbers still worked. Always keep the comps in mind when it comes to the scale of your renovation.

You don't always need to do a full-scale renovation unless the other sales in the neighborhood have been fully renovated.

2. Next, we have the old debate of being the project manager yourself or hiring a general contractor. Unless the job is small, I almost always prefer to hire a general contractor, even though there are pros and cons to each.

If you come from a construction background, then you could save some money by overseeing the project yourself and hiring out the different HVAC, electrical, plumbing, and other contractors that are needed. General contractors usually cost around 10% more.

That being said, if you can find a good general

contractor, they can save you a lot of time and headache since they will essentially be your project manager. In a later section of this guide, we go over how to find the best contractors.

You will still have to oversee them and make sure they are hitting their timelines and cost estimates, but it should save you some time so that you can find more properties.

3. The third thing to keep in mind is the area you live in and the finishes that are required in that specific area. One neighborhood versus another neighborhood can be drastically different.

In an area where homes sell over a million, a full kitchen might be 40 or 50K, while in another part of town a kitchen could be as little as 10K.

You want to look at the comps to make sure you are not overdoing it or underdoing it for your specific area.

The great thing about real estate, though, is that nowadays all the comp information on previous sales in your neighborhood are available online on sites like Redfin, Zillow, and others and include pictures of the properties and their level of finishes.

Study the comps online so that you know what level of renovation you will need to do. You can also get great ideas for what types of renovations to do by looking at past and actives sales in your same neighborhood.

4. You will improve. When you are first getting started with repair estimates, it can seem intimidating. However, after doing a few estimates and using some of the strategies in this book, you become an expert in estimating repair costs.

Even once you gain a level of comfort with estimating repairs, you should always seek out further knowledge through books like this, other real estate investors, training events, talking with contractors, and anything you can do.

There is always something you can learn from other successful investors when it comes to estimating repairs.

5. The fifth thing to keep in mind when doing repair estimates is that this should not take hours and hours. If I am meeting with a seller or walking through a property, it will usually take under 15 minutes. In fact, many times I will just take photos of the property and then go through the repair estimator sheet later filling in the info.

   The last thing you want to do is spend hours or days going through your repair estimator before getting back to the seller. If you have a motivated seller, you often times need to make them an offer the same day.

   Fortunately, once you get the process down for estimating repairs, you will be able to come up with a number in under 15 minutes.

6. When estimating repairs, you will never be 100% correct, and that is ok. The idea with the repair estimate is to get in the general ballpark of renovation cost. You just don't want to be the investor who is off by 50% on their amount.

   Also, it would be near impossible to be 100%

correct on any repair estimate because of all the variables in any rehab. The strategy I use that we will go over in this guide is to use a repair estimator which has about 25 different line items and then to add 10% to the total cost that I come up with.

7. Lastly, you should be using the MAO or maximum allowable offer formula for your offers. Coming up with a repair estimate is part of the MAO formula and works like this. MAO equals the after renovated value times .7 minus the cost of repairs.

So if a property will sell for 300K renovated and needed 50K worth of repairs, you would take 300K times .7 minus 50K which would give you 160K as the most you should offer for a property.

Okay, so there you have it, seven things to keep in mind when coming up with your repair estimate. In the next section, we go over the three main ways of estimating repairs accurately.

SECTION 2

3 WAYS OF ESTIMATING REPAIRS

When it comes to estimating repairs, there are really 3 different ways of doing it, some which are better than others. Each method has its own pros and cons which we will go over. The best way is to have a repair estimator sheet, even though some investors prefer to do a cost per square foot average, while others like to do a ballpark lump sum number.

For starters, I would recommend using a repair estimator sheet which you can download for free on my website www.jeff-leighton.com. In another section, we will discuss how you can tell if something needs to be replaced or not, but a general rule of thumb is to err on the conservative side and have it replaced.

The repair estimator is great because it includes all of the major components of a property in a line item format.

In addition, once you fill out the repair estimate, there will be an extra 10% added to the construction costs for overages. And, in almost every scenario, your actual repair cost will be more than your estimate. Keep that in mind and don't be surprised.

The repair estimator helps you get a close estimate, because the last thing you want to do as a newer investor is to be way off with your estimate. Ask me how I know.

You can take the sheet with you when looking at houses or just make a note and take pictures while you are at the property and then calculate everything later. You also should not be spending hours on this document.

In fact, it should be done within the time frame of a simple walk-through of the property. When in doubt, mark the item as needing to be replaced. You will have a pretty good basis for renovation costs after completing this document.

When I was a newer investor, I used to do repair estimate walk-throughs for a more experienced investor who would send me to 10 properties per day.

I would send him my repair estimate sheet as well as any notes, and he would have a great idea of the property condition and repairs needed. After doing a few walk-throughs, you will get it down.

Another way of estimating repairs is on a per square foot basis. When doing a complete gut renovation or building a new construction property, experienced investors tend to do more per square foot estimates. Some investors I know will estimate around 100 up to 150 per square foot for higher-end renovations and new construction in high-end areas.

While this is a viable strategy, I would only recommend this for more advanced investors. The cost per square foot method varies drastically for each area, type of property, level of finishes, and more.

The way most investors come up with their per square foot model is from direct experience of doing numerous rehabs and new construction projects. I would not use this method until you have done numerous deals.

Many investors, including myself, have started with smaller projects and worked their way up to large projects. I also can't emphasize enough that I would not start with a massive project as one of your first couple of deals unless you come from a construction background.

With larger projects, the likelihood of things going wrong is significantly higher. There are also plenty of smaller deals that you can start with to gain experience.

The last way of estimating repairs is to do a ballpark estimate. For example, if you know how much a style of home costs to renovate fully, you can just say that it will be 75K or 50K or 150K. Investors that do a lot of deals often know exactly how much a property will cost without even seeing the inside of the house.

You will learn how to come up with ballpark estimates by talking with other real estate investors at REIA (Real Estate Investor Association) meetings and real estate meetup groups.

This is again an advanced strategy and one that you can still use in some capacity. If you know investors in your area typically spend X amount on a property, you can use that as a reference and then calculate your own estimate with the repair estimate sheet.

Nowadays, while I prefer to see a property in person, I can make offers over the phone because I know exactly how much a house will cost to renovate.

So there you have it, the three main ways of estimating repairs. They can all be used to some extent, but I would recommend that all newer investors use a repair estimator.

Also, when in doubt, ask a more experienced local investor who you know, like, and trust. And don't feel bashful about asking a more experienced investor, they can give you a ballpark estimate. They usually love to help newer investors who are up and coming because they were in the same position when they began their career.

SECTION 3

HOW TO BECOME A CONSTRUCTION EXPERT

In the next section, we go over actual estimate ranges for each part of the house so you can have a general idea of costs and come up with an estimate.

That being said, you should always attempt to learn how to estimate repairs and improve your construction knowledge. I learned how to estimate repairs in a few ways, so you will become an expert at repairs in no time.

When I was a rookie real estate investor, I had no idea how much different repairs cost. I didn't know if a kitchen was 10K or 100K since I had heard both estimates at one time or another. If you watch Million Dollar Listing, which is a great show, you might think that a renovation costs 500K, but most likely that is not applicable to your area. In some areas, you can do a full house renovation for less than 50K.

Fortunately, there are simple ways to further your construction knowledge in addition to reading guides like this. The first thing I did was join every single real estate investor association (REIA) and real estate investing Meetup I could. I would make a note to listen and ask other investors what the cost of repairs for different properties was.

The great thing about these meetings is that they always profile local members' deals they have going on and how much they expected to pay in rehab costs vs. how much they actually paid.

Sometimes, the Meetup groups even gather at the property being rehabbed so you can look at the deal in person. Once you hear a few case studies and start talking to other investors at these groups, you will begin to hear trends and ballpark numbers for what it costs to rehab in your area. This is very helpful and you should make notes of this.

The next best way to learn about construction is to do online research. There are plenty of home repair estimate sites like HomeAdvisor.com and others that will tell you exactly how much the fix will be depending on your zip code.

These sites often give you a low, medium, and high estimate, which can be very helpful depending on the type of neighborhood you are in.

Lastly, if you have built up your list of contractors, which is simple and easy to do and will be covered in a later section of this guide, you should pay them for an hour of their time to walk through a house with you and give you an estimate.

If you have a good rapport with the contractors or know a friend or family member who is a contractor, they will probably do it for free.

Just tell them you are looking to get a better understanding of a property. You can also just take them out to lunch and show them some pictures of a property and get them to give you ballpark prices and ask them what their last renovation projects cost.

If you took a few investors or contractors out to lunch, you would soon have a great idea of good ballpark prices for construction.

So there you have it, in addition to reading this guide a couple of times, you should also use the aforementioned strategies to further your construction knowledge.

Even though I have a lot of real estate investing experience, I still seek out further knowledge and information on construction best practices and prices. You should too.

That being said, you should always attend local investing Meetups to hear what investors are paying for renovations, do your own research online, and take contractors out to lunch or to walk a property or two with them. I've used all of the aforementioned strategies and still do in many cases.

You should never stop learning. In fact, I recently met up with an investor who had almost 20 projects actively going on and who was still asking me questions about real estate investing, even though he was much more accomplished.

Keep an open mind and always look for additional information that can help you become a more informed investor when it comes to repairs or anything else.

SECTION 4

EXTERIOR COST ESTIMATES

In this section, we are going over the main exterior components of a house renovation and what you need to keep in mind when coming up with your estimate. We will go over how to tell if something needs to be replaced versus repaired.

Also, this section will give you real numbers that you can use, including a low estimate and a high estimate, so you have a range to work with. Keep in mind these estimates are for houses under one million.

Once you get in the million-dollar price range, the prices can shoot up because of the size and particulars of a high-end renovation. These are all estimates, so depending on the price range and size of your property, you should decide whether to go with the lower or higher estimate.

1. **Roof:** Roofs can be a significant expense for an investor depending on the complexity of the roof

and the size of the house. For a small townhouse, I would not be too worried if the roof needed to be replaced because of the size. However, with a large single-family house, a roof can add up quickly. The way you know you should replace a roof is pretty straightforward.

There are a couple of things to look for. Is the roof showing signs of the shingles curling, cracking, or does it have missing shingles? Does the roof have multiple layers of shingles? Is the roof covered in moss and does it look deteriorated? If you see these issues, then it probably means you should replace the roof.

Generally speaking, it is not difficult to determine whether or not you need to replace the roof. Would a reasonable person look at the roof and say it's in good condition or poor condition?

Take a look at your roof in comparison to other roofs in the neighborhood. At the end of the day, when selling your rehab, you want your roof to look the best in the neighborhood, in addition to interior work.

COST ESTIMATE: The cost to replace a townhouse roof would be about 7K. For a larger single-family house or higher-end detached home, you could easily be at 15K or 25K. Estimate 7K-25K. If you are not sure, 10K is a good starting point. The more complicated and the more ridges and structure to a roof, the more expensive it will be.

2. **Gutters:** Next up are your gutters. While you may not think they are that big of a deal, gutters play a big role in preventing water issues and keeping water away from the house. Damaged or hanging gutters are also a massive eyesore and will kill any chances of curb appeal with your property.

   How do you know if you need to replace your gutters? Are the gutters sagging and pulling away from the house? Are the gutters dented, bent, or cracked? Are the gutters filled with water or debris and do they generally look like they are in bad condition? Fortunately, gutters are not that expensive to repair or to replace completely.

   COST ESTIMATE: I would budget $500-$5000 depending on how many gutters you have and the complexity of the gutter system. Also, many times you may just have to repair the gutters and not replace them.

3. **Siding:** Siding is a repair that can really make the house shine. Generally, you only need to replace siding on older houses. What you need to look for with siding are damaged pieces, outdated colors, and rotting or warped pieces. If there are just a few places that have damage, you may be able to paint and replace those pieces.

However, if your siding looks really old and in bad condition, then plan on a full replacement. One thing to note is that if your house has asbestos siding, then you should plan on paying extra for a company to encapsulate it and properly remove the siding.

Homes from the 1950s can have asbestos siding. Look up a picture online of what asbestos siding looks like. It is very distinctive and easy to recognize.

COST ESTIMATE: Plan on spending 5K-20K for a full replacement of your siding. If it is just missing pieces here and there, then you probably only have to pay a few hundred to a few thousand.

4. **Windows:** Windows are a part of the house that every buyer will look for. You need to make sure the windows are operable and look great. Every now and then, I will buy a rehab where the previous owner updated the windows to nicer vinyl windows.

   Generally, though, the windows need to be replaced. Many times, windows are painted shut or cracked in different places. By replacing the windows, you can get more for your house and have the property looking great, even though windows are not cheap.

   COST ESTIMATE: I would budget $250-$400 per window for a full replacement with a nice, modern vinyl window.

5. **Exterior Paint:** One of the simplest things you can do to give your house a boost in curb appeal is give it a fresh coat of paint. When deciding on a good paint color, you never want to go too extreme. Instead, go with a nice neutral color.

I like to drive around the neighborhood and look at the comps online to find a couple of similar houses with attractive exterior paint colors and then decide.

In fact, that goes for just about every exterior and interior renovation. Just look at which neighbors and comps have the best ideas and then use those for your property.

COST ESTIMATE: Expect to pay around $2-$3 per square foot for a house. In other words, it would cost about $2,500 to paint the exterior of a smaller, 1200-square-foot home. I would budget $2,500-$7,000 to paint the exterior depending on the size of your house.

6. **Landscaping:** Landscaping is a must for any rehab project. This can make a great first impression on potential buyers and make your house stand out. Fortunately, landscaping is not a huge investment of time or money.

   Just doing the basics such as trimming hedges, mowing the lawn or putting in sod, and adding mulch can have a significant impact. In a later section of this guide, I have a curb appeal checklist with 15 items to keep in mind.

COST ESTIMATE: For landscaping, you can plan to spend at least $1,000 and up to $5,000 depending on the extent of the project and size of the lot. If you need to remove large trees that are right on top of the property, expect to pay several thousand per tree.

7. **Garage:** If your property has a garage, then you need to make sure it is up to par with the rest of the house. There are some simple upgrades that are not expensive and can make your garage stand out. For starters, you should remove all items from the garage and clean it out as much as possible.

   Next, you can do this yourself or hire a garage company to put a professional floor coating on the garage floor which acts as a sealant and looks great.

   After that, you can paint the garage a nice light color such as white. Lastly, you should replace the garage door if it's in bad condition.

According to Realtor.com, replacing the garage door has the best return on investment of any renovation project, so don't skimp on that.

COST ESTIMATE: A complete garage renovation, including brand new door, floor sealant, interior paint, trashing everything out, and replacing any light fixtures, will cost around $5,000 total. If you are just cleaning out, re-surfacing, and re-painting, then it should be only a few thousand.

8. **Pools:** A pool is one of those amenities that some people love and some hate. It all depends on what part of the country you are in. In my area on the east coast, I rarely come across pools, but in some parts of the country, pools are everywhere.

If the pool looks like it's in rough condition and has visible cracks, then factor in some repairs. Many times you don't need to be a pool expert to know that a pool needs work.

You also might have to replace various types of equipment for the pool, such as the pump and heater or re-plastering over leaks in the pool.

COST ESTIMATE: If the pool looks like it's in rough condition and has visible cracks, then it could easily cost a couple thousand and as much as 5K to get it in working condition.

9. **Fence:** Having a fence or removing an old dilapidated fence can make a big difference for curb appeal. There is nothing like a brand new fence, and many buyers prefer the privacy that comes with a quality fence.

   If the property currently does not have a fence, then I would look around at the neighbors' houses to see who has the nicest-looking fence and then model that one.

   COST ESTIMATE: While there are different styles of fences, including wood, metal, and vinyl, you should plan on about $10-$15 per linear foot of fence. In other words, for a quarter acre lot of about 200 linear feet, you would be paying around $2K-6K.

10. **Deck:** A deck can be a great selling point to a house. If the home already has a deck, it will most likely need some additional repairs and finishing

to be ready for the next buyer. The regulations and code on decks change all the time, and it would be a good idea to get a deck repair company to evaluate the deck.

Typical repairs include staining and sealing the deck with a fresh new coat of sealer, anchoring deck stairs, replacing deck boards, removing popped out nails, and replacing rotten posts.

COST ESTIMATE: Depending on how much work the deck needs, I would estimate $500 to $2,500 to get the deck in good condition. If you are installing a new deck, be prepared to spend 5K for a smaller wood deck up to 20K for a large composite deck. Deck installation is another item that is always on the list of best ROI for renovations when doing a property.

11. **Septic**: If you are further outside of a city, the property might be on a septic system. Before you buy any house with a septic tank, you must get it inspected since they can be costly to replace.

    If the property is listed on the market, then the seller will typically have to hire a company to check it out. If I am buying an off-market deal I will usually pay out of pocket to get a septic inspection.

COST ESTIMATE: It's going to cost about $250-$500 for a septic inspection but could save you a fortune. If a septic system is in bad condition it could cost you anywhere from a few thousand dollars up to 15K. And keep in mind, most properties will not be on septic.

If the septic company say it needs a certain number of repairs, then you should put that on the seller to credit you before closing or to have them pay the septic company directly from the proceeds of the sale.

12. **Demo/Dumpsters:** When you buy a house, one of the first things you have to do is trash out the place and start demoing. When working with motivated sellers, I let them know they can leave whatever they want in the house to make it a hassle-free transaction for them.

Fortunately, there are plenty of trash and junk removal vendors. I would recommend getting a couple of quotes and making sure you use a licensed company for liability reasons.

COST ESTIMATE: Depending on whether the place is a smaller condo, a townhome or a larger single-family home, I would estimate $500 up to $3K.

SECTION 5

INTERIOR COST ESTIMATES

Now that we got the exterior estimates done, let's head inside and run numbers on the interior renovations.

1. **Kitchen:** Kitchen renovations are crucial to selling a property. Sometimes you can just replace the appliances, paint, and add some nice backsplash. However, if the kitchen is completely outdated, you will need to do an entire kitchen renovation.

   Curb appeal, kitchens, and bathrooms are three of the biggest things buyers notice, so make sure to invest some time and money into your kitchen.

   If the property is not that old and the kitchen is in good condition then you may just need to do some updates. You want to get an idea of the comps and see what the top selling properties in that neighborhood have sold for and do your renovation accordingly.

COST ESTIMATE: For a small condo, expect to start at around 10K for a full kitchen renovation. The cost goes up to 15K-35K for a single-family house kitchen renovation. Adjust accordingly for the size and price range of your property.

2. **Layout:** If you are rehabbing a property built before 1990, then there's a good chance you may need to open up some of the walls to have a better layout. Buyers these days prefer as much open flow to the house as possible.

   What you may not realize is that you are able to open up non-loadbearing walls as well as loadbearing walls when necessary. There are ways of opening up nearly any space. Just make sure you have a licensed and insured contractor. They may need to bring in their architect and engineer to confirm opening up some walls.

   COST ESTIMATE: Expect to pay about 2K upwards of 10K to remove a loadbearing wall if the home has several levels. Removing a non-loadbearing wall is relatively simple and should cost less than 1K. Always check with an engineer or licensed contractor before removing any walls, just to be sure.

3. **Bathrooms:** When renovating a house, you must renovate or at least update the bathrooms. Besides the kitchen, the bathrooms also play a big role in any buyer's decision.

   At the very least, you should update outdated bath and light fixtures, painting, and putting in a new vanity. And if you are on a tight budget and can only afford to do one bathroom, then make sure you renovate the master bathroom.

   Pick designs and finishes that are in line with comparable sales. If you don't specify with your contractor the exact style and photos of what you want your bathroom to look like, they could end up choosing the cheapest Home Depot supplies. Ask me how I know…

   COST ESTIMATE: Expect to pay 5K to 15K for a full bathroom renovation. If it's just a half bath, then the costs should only be about $2.5K to $5K.

4. **Flooring:** Flooring can make or break a sale. This is another part of the renovation where you need

to stay up to date on what is popular in your area. For example, in some hip, upscale neighborhoods you won't find carpet anywhere. In other areas, it can be more prevalent. Try to match the top-selling comps with the same type of flooring. Do not cheap out on this part.

You should go through the highest sold comparable properties in your area and make a list of what type of flooring they had in different part of the house. Hardwood floors throughout the living area and tile in the bathrooms are usually a good bet, but always check.

You can often refinish older hardwood floors and make them look great. Buyers often appreciate keeping some of the historic charm of an older property.

COST ESTIMATE: Hardwood floors usually cost about $7-$15 per square foot to install. If you are just refinishing the floors, then expect to pay $2-$6 per square foot. Installing tile is similar and will be in the $7-$15 range. If you are replacing carpet, expect to be in the $2-$5 per square foot range.

5. **Drywall/Sheetrock:** Drywall and/or sheetrock repairs are common in most properties. At the very least, you will need drywall patching throughout the property. In some cases, you may need to replace it entirely. Drywall repairs would be considered more of a minor repair than some of the other items we have gone over.

   However, you still want to make sure your drywall contractor is a specialist because there is nothing worse than a cheaply done drywall job with the tape exposed and small cracks throughout the finishes.

   COST ESTIMATE: Expect to pay around $500 per room if you need to replace the drywall. Most homes however do not need a full replacement unless they are in seriously bad condition. Drywall repair in general is not that expensive and relatively easy for a contractor to do. You should estimate around $50 - $70 per square foot for drywall repair.

6. **HVAC and Hot Water Heater:** It is common on most rehabs that the HVAC and hot water heater are past their useful life expectancy and need to be

replaced. This can be a bigger ticket item, especially the HVAC.

To find out the age of the HVAC and hot water heater, look at the serial number on the units. The 3rd and 4th digit of the serial number is often the year it was installed. For example, if the serial number is 3506XXXX, then the heater was installed in 2006.

Every unit and manufacturer can vary. If you can't read the number and the system looks old and rusted, then it's a good idea to replace it. Keep in mind that most systems only last about 15 years.

In some cases, with systems less than 10 years old, you may not even need to replace them as long as they are working fine. Instead, you could just get a tune-up from your local HVAC company.

COST ESTIMATE: To replace a furnace and AC unit, expect to pay around $3,500 - $5000 for each. You will spend about 7K-10K for a full HVAC replacement. A hot water heater usually runs around $1K-2K.

7. **Plumbing:** When buying a house, you should

assume that every home could use some plumbing updates. There is always preventive maintenance and small plumbing fixes that can be done throughout the property to make sure it's running well.

Some of these include repairing leaky joints, replacing shut-off valves, low water pressure, slow drains, and ensuring the sump pump works. Typically, these are considered normal or standard updates that should not cost you more than a couple of hours of a plumber's time.

In terms of replacing parts or the entire plumbing system, that is something you and your contractor will have to determine. If there are numerous places throughout the house where the plumbing is not working correctly and the house is old, i.e., built before 1950, then the pipes might need to be replaced.

Homes built in the mid-20th century should have exposed pipes in the basement where you can get a good look at them. Sometimes they are in excellent condition, while other times they are clearly not working correctly and you can see visible leaks and corrosion. Additionally, it's not uncommon for vacant properties to have the copper pipes stolen from them.

In either of these scenarios, it's probably best to start over and replace the pipes completely. Again, you only need to replace pipes on older houses. In homes built after 1960 or 1970, you can often just repair them as needed.

Lastly, in some houses, you will need to add a bathroom in the basement or another section of the house. Having enough bathrooms can get you top resale value once the home is renovated. Consider this if your house does not have enough bathrooms.

COST ESTIMATE: Expect to pay $5K-15K to replace the pipes for a large, older house. If you are adding a bathroom in the house, I would factor $5K-20K for a full bathroom installation. If the home is newer, it will most likely only need minor updates and repairs in the ballpark of $1K-5K.

8. **Electrical:** Nearly every house I come across has

electrical work that could and should be done. With rehabs you always want to try to add lights when possible and you must also factor in replacing all the switches, outlets, and light fixtures.

Those simple renovations will give your property a much cleaner and more modern look. Additionally, you will want to consider upgrading the service panel if it's 100 amps or less.

Newer homes are built with 200 amp panels, to give you an idea. Every now and then, you will run across a house that needs to be re-wired entirely, which can get expensive.

There is no real way to tell without bringing in an electrician, but if it's an older house, the electrical panel is a mess, and you see other signs like charred outlets and switches, then you should add re-wiring to the budget.

COST ESTIMATE: Expect to pay $7K-20K to re-wire a house, depending on the size. Keep in mind that the majority of homes don't need to be re-wired. Upgrading the panel is in the ballpark of

$2K-3K and can make the house seem much more modern and appealing to the end buyer. The cost of updating and replacing all the outlets, switches, and light fixtures should be in the ballpark of $1,500-$3,000.

9. **Carpentry (Trim and Molding)**: To really make your property stand out when you go to sell, the trim work around windows, doors, and moldings should have nice tight sharp corners. This is a simple yet overlooked repair that can give your property that extra boost to stand out.

   COST ESTIMATE: Replacing the trim and molding is in the ballpark of $1K to 5K. If you get really high-end with the crown molding, you can expect double that price.

10. **Termites:** Termites can be an issue in some parts of the country, particularly in the south and southwest. They like wooden structures such as porches, decks, garages, as well as any damp areas near a property.

    Since your end buyer will do a termite inspection as a requirement of their loan, you should pay for a termite inspection and do any necessary repairs to be proactive.

COST ESTIMATE: If you need just a basic treatment and repair, expect to pay around $500. However, if there is a larger termite issue, you could spend as much as $2,000-$5,000. In my experience in the mid-Atlantic area, significant termite damage is very rare.

11. **Interior Paint:** The interior of 100% of the houses you buy and renovate will need to be painted. Always go with a lighter, neutral color. This is not the time to experiment with colors you've never tried before.

    Make sure to paint not just the walls but also the ceilings and trim work. This will make your property stand out and show that you don't cut corners.

    COST ESTIMATE: Expect to pay around $3-$6 per square foot when you paint the interior of the house. I would highly recommend hiring someone to do this. Just because you painted your room one time does not qualify you to paint an entire house so that you can save a few thousand dollars. Hire a professional and get it done right. It will save you a ton of time and headaches.

12. **Mold:** Mold is another issue you will run into in some properties. Fortunately, mold is typically easier to remediate than most would have you believe. In fact, one of my investor friends preferred to buy houses with mold because it scared everyone away and he knew he could remove it affordably.

Mold is often a result of bad grading on the exterior of the house. The process for removing the mold issue typically involves spraying the areas with mold killer and then cutting any drywall that is affected. Mold removal companies will also have an air filtration vacuum.

After removing the mold, they will either improve the grading with landscaping or in some cases install a French drain or sump pump. In rare cases, a basement waterproofing company will install a full waterproofing system.

COST ESTIMATE: Always consult a

professional mold removal company, but expect to pay anywhere from $500 for a little bit of mold up to $10K for serious mold throughout the house. If you are unsure about the mold, then you should probably not buy the house. A full waterproofing system for a basement can run anywhere from $2K to $10K and they typically come with a lifetime warranty.

13. **Permits:** As an investor, you should also factor in the cost of permits. You should also become well versed in the permit process so that you can get work done quickly and for the best price. The last thing you want to do is ignore permits and try to take shortcuts on the job.

    If you have done a significant renovation, the first thing any potential buyer will ask is, what contractor did the work and did they pull permits? You want to be sure you can easily answer that question so make sure to hire a licensed contractor who pulls necessary permits.

    COST ESTIMATE: Permits will cost anywhere from $250 up to $3K if there is a lot of work involved. Depending on the scale of your project you should estimate accordingly.

14. **Insulation**: A nice selling feature is having upgraded insulation. Most older homes do not have the proper amount of insulation, and you don't want to have a buyer come back three months after you sold them the house complaining that it's cold. Insulation is also usually easy to install.

    COST ESTIMATE: For adding insulation to a property you should factor on at least $500 and upwards of $5000 if it's an older, larger house.

In this section, we covered the main components of any renovation. Like I mentioned, budget on the conservative side if you are not sure. In addition, once we add up our number, we always add a minimum 10% cost to any rehab project, just to be sure.

These estimates will get you right in the ballpark of the actual costs of a project. For older houses or large homes over 4,000 square feet, you will have to keep your budget on the conservative side and add at least 15% to your rehab budget.

SECTION 6

HELPFUL RULES OF THUMB

In this section, we will go over 9 rules of thumb when it comes to estimating repairs that you must understand. These principles are universally true for a beginner investor or even an experienced investor.

Rule of Thumb #1: For starters, the older the house, the more repairs you will need to do. I know that sounds simple enough, but with older homes, there could be a lot of unknowns that you are not even aware of when you first see the property.

When you open up the drywall, you might find things you were not expecting, like a faulty electrical system, leaking plumbing, and more. That's why condo fees at older buildings are so high versus newer condos: they have significantly more maintenance to deal with.

Rule of Thumb #2: The next principle is that the larger and more complicated your rehab project is, the more conservative you need to be. There is a big difference between doing a simple townhouse cosmetic fix and flip versus doing a two-story addition on a single-family house and digging out the basement so that it can be finished off.

If you are new to real estate, I would never recommend doing a massive project like that as your first deal just because there is so much more that can go wrong and costs can get out of control.

Always start out with a smaller project and work your way up to large projects. The larger projects should be the most profitable, but you need to make sure you have the experience to take on something like that.

Rule of Thumb #3: Do not rely on estimates from others. If a wholesaler or real estate agent tells you that the property needs only 30K worth of work, make sure you verify that number yourself.

On paper, a deal can look great, but real estate agents and especially wholesalers have a well-deserved reputation for inflating numbers or not accurately estimating repairs.

I am always skeptical of other people's repair estimates and have seen many cases where their estimates are off by more than double. That's not to say there are no good deals from wholesalers and real estate agents. You can find amazing deals, but make sure you always do your own due diligence.

Rule of Thumb #4: When coming up with your repair estimate, always add 10 percent to your grand total. If you want to make profitable deals, then make sure you are adding at least 10 percent to your rehab estimate. The repair estimator I have on my website has that built in and it's a pretty simple formula either way.

Additionally, if you are doing a large project over 100K in repairs, then I would recommend you add at least 15% to your construction budget.

Even after having been in the business for a while, I still add that amount to the total for unexpected costs. Nearly every rehab will have some type of surprise or something you overlooked.

Rule of Thumb #5: Every now and then, you will have to make an estimate on repairs for a property that you have never seen the interior of. I have bought several houses like that, and there are a couple things to keep in mind. You should drive by the outside of the house and try to get a look at the foundation and sides of the house.

Most homes do not have major foundation issues, but usually you can get a good idea of the house just by looking at the exterior. Then factor in that the house will need a full gut renovation. There is a chance that the property won't need that much work, but it's better to stay on the safe side.

Rule of Thumb #6: This is the golden rule of estimating repairs and renovating properties. Always get three bids for your job. I don't care if you have the best contractor of all time. To keep them honest and possibly find a better contractor you always need three bids.

Just make sure they know exactly what you are looking to do because I've seen repair bids come in all over the place when people are not crystal clear about the scope of work they are looking to get done.

Rule of Thumb #7: Use the MAO or maximum allowable offer formula for all of your deals. When getting started in real estate investing, it can be tempting to think every other house that needs work is a good deal. In reality, when you use the MAO formula, you will quickly eliminate about 90 percent of the deals out there.

The MAO formula takes into account your repair estimate and your after renovated value and spits out precisely the number you would need to offer for a profitable deal.

This formula will help you even if your repair estimate is slightly off because of how conservative a number it is. The way it works is you take the after renovated value and multiply it by .7, and then subtract for the cost of repairs.

That number is the most you should pay for a property. So if a property sells for 300K renovated and needs 50K worth of work, you would multiply 300 times .7 minus 50K, and you would get 160K as your maximum offer price.

Although you can go above .7 when it comes to higher-priced homes, I would recommend sticking to this formula until you have built up a lot of experience.

Rule of Thumb #8: When it comes to estimating repairs and the actual construction, your project will cost more and take longer than you were planning. Now, that's not to say that your deals can't be immensely profitable, but it's just something you should expect going in.

Once you get into a rehab, there will be things you might want to do differently or add to the project. That is okay, as long as you plan on some variables before going into the deal.

Rule of Thumb #9: Lastly, when it comes to choosing a contractor for your job, I usually prefer a general contractor. A GC is more expensive than if you just hire electricians, plumber, carpenters, etc., but having a good GC manage the project for you can save you tons of time and headache.

By having a good GC, you can have multiple projects going on at once and not lose your mind. You can consider managing smaller projects yourself, but for larger projects, I would recommend letting the experts handle it.

SECTION 7

REPAIRS THAT ADD THE MOST VALUE

In this section, we will go over what repairs add the most value and what you should try to focus on doing. It's incredible to me how some owners will renovate a property only to have it be less appealing than it was before. Focus on these repairs to get the best return on investment.

The first thing you should do is make sure the curb appeal is top of the line. I have been into hundreds, if not thousands, of homes and curb appeal makes a massive difference.

First impressions are everything in real estate. Curb appeal is also easy to implement and not very expensive to do, so there is no reason not to focus on this. Depending on your budget, this is a checklist of items to do for curb appeal. These 15 inexpensive items will instantly give potential buyers a better impression of your property.

1. Mow the lawn and trim the hedges
2. Paint the exterior
3. Plant flowers or put them in flower pots
4. Power-wash your front patio area
5. Clean or replace the windows
6. Replace the entry door or buy an upgraded handle
7. Replace the garage door
8. Install a modern doorbell
9. Ensure gutters are clean and in proper alignment
10. Add upgraded light fixtures in the front-of-house entryway
11. Replace house number
12. Repair/Replace or paint shutters
13. Make sure your walkway is in good condition and repair or add lighting as needed
14. Repaint or replace the mailbox
15. Clean up your yard as much as possible

The next part of your renovation that can give you the best ROI is opening up space as much as possible. For whatever reason, older homes were built with many rooms and walls and can make the property feel much smaller than it is. Have your licensed contractor evaluate and try to open up the space as much as possible.

Many times, it is much easier than you would think to open up a space. Buyers nowadays are looking for open and modern homes. In fact, I just sold a property that I completely rehabbed, but I did not open it up because it was a townhome.

The house next door sold for 30K more than mine and was not even fully renovated, but it was open. That was the main difference buyers were looking for.

The third thing you should focus on is going lighter and more modern. That means nice light neutral paint and floors, as well as focusing on a modern touch throughout with things like light fixtures and door handles.

If you can add more natural light to the property, then do that as well by replacing older doors or even adding a skylight.

One of my associates just did a small yet impactful renovation on a condo they were selling. It was a condo, so it was not a massive renovation, but it made a big difference and got the property sold quickly when the first listing agent could not sell it.

They replaced the main light fixtures in the unit with brighter and more modern fixtures, installed a modern thermostat, painted the property a lighter neutral color, and replaced the door fixtures with a modern style. All of these inexpensive repairs made the property really pop, and they quickly got an offer and sold it.

Overall, if you focus on curb appeal, opening up space, and then going for a lighter/modern feel, you should be in a great position to get your property sold fast with a nice ROI.

That being said, according to HGTV and Fixr, the top ten home renovations with the best ROI also include kitchen, bathrooms, new windows, new appliances, decks, siding, and roof.

I would recommend focusing on the basics of what buyers are looking for and trying not to do anything out of line with where the neighborhood comps are. Before doing your renovation, you should have a good idea of what different properties in that neighborhood have done and try to model the best ideas that you've seen.

SECTION 8

TOP MISTAKES WHEN ESTIMATING REPAIRS

There are some common mistakes when it comes to estimating repairs that you must be aware of. I have literally made all of these mistakes, and I can tell you by reading this section thoroughly you will be able to save a lot of money and headaches.

1. The first mistake is that when people are creating an estimate, they are often not aware of the finishes and renovations of similar style homes.

   For example, in some areas, the highest-priced homes might not even be renovated at all. Instead, they might all be in livable condition. That means you might be making a big mistake by doing a full-scale renovation, when instead you could do more cosmetic items and still get a great ROI.

   Or for example, in other areas, all of the comps might be very high-end renovations. If you did a middle-of-the-road or low-end renovation, your property would stick out like a sore thumb.

The reverse is true as well. I have seen some investors go into a low-price neighborhood and try to build the Taj Mahal of rehab projects with marble floors and what not.

You can waste a lot of money by going over the top on your project and not understanding what similar properties have done as far as renovations. Make sure to study online or, even better, check out open houses of similar homes in the area to get an idea for your finishes.

2. Another mistake that I wanted to reiterate is that I see a lot of rehabbers relying on estimates from others, including real estate agents, wholesalers, or even sellers in some cases. Wholesalers will almost always send you a deal that looks great on paper but in reality, their construction numbers can be way off.

That is not to say you can't find amazingly lucrative deals from wholesalers, but take their numbers with a grain of salt.

I've found real estate agent estimates to be much closer, although still a bit lower than the actual estimate. Unless that agent is actively doing deals themselves or unless you have worked with them in the past, then I would always try to verify the numbers yourself.

Most of the time, sellers underestimate the costs of the repairs. Selling a house can be an emotional time, and they might not want to tell you the entire home needs to be renovated.

However, the good thing about repair estimates is that once you do a couple and start doing rehabs, you will soon learn exactly what different styles of properties need without even having to spend too much time.

3. A third mistake I see a lot of newer real estate investors make is that they take forever to come up with a repair estimate. Keep in mind that this is an estimate, not an exact number. The goal is not to be 100% correct; the goal is just to not be off by a significant amount.

   I remember showing a property a while ago to

some "investors" who spent almost an hour at the house examining every closet and taking pictures of the landscaping and other trivial items.

This is a complete waste of time, and an experienced investor would never do this. A repair estimate should be a 15-minute walk-through of the property, noting the items that need work. And if you aren't sure, just take a picture and mark the item as needing to be replaced.

The last thing you want to do is lose a deal because you took too long to get back to the seller about your offer. Some investors want to get several estimates before even making an offer. Good deals never last, so be sure to do a conservative estimate if you are not sure and get back to the motivated seller ASAP with an offer.

4. While investors tend to underestimate repairs, I do sometimes see newer investors who overestimate repairs. How do I know? Well, when I was getting started, I was on the super conservative side of things and missed out on many great deals because I overestimated repairs.

Here is what I want to tell you. If you are unsure of whether or not a property is a good deal, reach out to a local investor who you know, like, and trust and ask them about their opinion.

Not everyone buys properties to do a complete renovation, so if the property is still priced as one of the lowest comps in the area, then chances are that deal has a lot of potential. More experienced investors might have a large buyers list of local investors that pay a premium for fixer-uppers.

Even to this day, when I'm not sure about the repair costs, I will still partner with a more experienced investor to wholesale the deal to one of their thousands of potential buyers.

5. Just ballparking a repair number. If you are an experienced investor, then you often know exactly how much a property will take to renovate.

   However, when getting started, I would be sure to use a repair estimator. If you try to just ballpark a number, you will almost certainly be wrong. Also, a repair estimator only takes a few minutes to fill out and is a helpful tool for anyone.

You would be surprised how many additional items you come up with when you have an actual repair estimator instead of a wild guess. After practicing with the repair estimator on different styles of properties, you should start to get an intuitive feel for how much a property will cost.

SECTION 9

HOW TO FIND
THE BEST CONTRACTORS

In this part, we will go over how to find the best contractors for rehabbing houses. Keep in mind that you should be aiming to build a list of good contractors instead of just finding one good contractor. Most investors are not strategic with making their list of contractors.

Sometimes contractors get busy with other projects, sometimes your contractor's quality of work may start going down, and you always need three bids on a project. Therefore, it's essential to have an "all-star" team of contractors. These strategies should make it fairly easy for you to create a list of at least 10 qualified, pre-vetted contractors.

1. My favorite way of finding contractors is simple and easy. Drive around in the neighborhood where you have bought a property or where you will be buying a property and look for contractor

yard signs.

I see countless yard signs and contractor trucks with the contact information of the company in just about any neighborhood I go to.

When you see these, you can write down the number and website and start building a list. You could quickly create a list of 5-10 contractors with this strategy alone.

It's a good sign when a contractor is working in your neighborhood since they will know those types of properties. Plus, you should be driving around the neighborhood anyway to get a good feel for the comps.

2. The next way to add names to your list of contractors is to ask for referrals from friends, family, real estate professionals, co-workers, and anyone else you can think of. People love recommending contractors if they did a great job. Sometimes they even go in depth to show you the before-and-after photos of the work they had done.

3. The websites of local real estate agents are another

great resource. What you can do is look up different real estate agents in your city and go to the "recommended vendors" or a similar section on their websites.

They will have a list of recommended title companies, lenders, and also contractors. While not every agent will have this, many of the top agents in your area should have a list of contractors they like to use. By just spending an hour or so online, you should be able to add even more qualified contractors to your list.

4. Another great way to find contractors is through Angie's List and Yelp. Angie's List is great because you can sign up for free and find discounted deals on contractor services as well as all the reviews from people who have used that service.

Angie's List also does a great job of prescreening the contractors for you. Yelp is not as good as Angie's List, but it's a good idea to check the Yelp reviews as well. Some contractors may not have Yelp, but I would still check. You want all the available information on a contractor.

5. Home Depot and other supply houses. If you go to Home Depot, Lowes, as well as specialty supply stores for electrical, HVAC, plumbing, and others you can ask for recommended contractors.

   The people at these stores should have no issues whatsoever recommending a few names to you. In fact, they should be happy to do so. It would only mean more business for them as well, since the contractors frequent their stores.

6. Lastly, you should be attending REIA (real estate investor association) meetings as well as real estate investing Meetup groups in your area. At these events, there will probably be contractors whose contact information you can get.

   Additionally, you can ask other investors there if they have any recommended contractors. They will probably give you recommended contractors as well as contractors to avoid.

These strategies should make it easy for you to build a list of at least 10 qualified, recommended contractors – if not 25. Keep in mind that some contractors might not be available all the time, so you need to have a large qualified list.

Before you pick your contractor, remember a few things. The best contractors are always busy, so you should be a little hesitant if the contractor does not seem to have too much going on.

Next, make sure your contractor is licensed and insured, which is something they should provide easily to you. Lastly, even after you have your qualified list of great contractors, you should still get three bids just to make sure everyone is on the same page.

And while nothing is ever guaranteed, by using those strategies to find contractors, you will maximize your likelihood of doing a successful rehab.

NOW IT'S YOUR TURN

Thanks for reading this guide. You should now have everything you need to start making educated estimates on construction repairs for your deals. Keep in mind that you will never be 100% correct on the estimate, but it will help you get right in the ballpark of the actual costs. I see far too many investors making uninformed estimates because they don't know any better.

I hope that you enjoyed this informative guide. I have tried to add as much value as possible.

If you enjoyed this book and found it useful, I'd be very grateful if you would leave an honest review.

Every review makes a difference, and I read and appreciate all feedback.

Thanks again.

Sincerely,

Jeff Leighton

ABOUT THE AUTHOR

Jeff Leighton is a real estate investor, real estate broker, and bestselling Amazon Author. He has been mentored by some of the top real estate investors in the US and continues to invest in real estate to this day.

Want More Training?

Go to **www.jeff-leighton.com** for helpful videos, free resources, downloads, additional mentoring, online programs, and much, much more. You can also text **DEAL to 345345** to stay updated on everything we have going on in the real estate investing world.

Other Books By The Author

Available on Amazon

Follow Jeff Leighton

Instagram.com/JeffRLeighton
YouTube.com/JeffLeighton1
Facebook.com/JeffLeighton5

Printed in Poland
by Amazon Fulfillment
Poland Sp. z o.o., Wrocław